Mithras Reader Vol.2

Sun Circle by Farangis Yegane.

An Academic and Religious Journal of Greek, Roman and Persian Studies.

Editor: Payam Nabarz

Papers and Contributions by: Dr. Israel Campos Méndez, Kim Huggens, Farangis Yegane, James Rodriguez, Jalil Nozari, Robert Kavjian, M. Hajduk, Harita Meenee, Farida Bamji, S David, Katherine Sutherland, and Payam Nabarz.

Mithras Reader: An Academic and Religious Journal of Greek, Roman and Persian Studies. Vol II.

ISBN-13: 978-0-9556858-1-1

Editor: Payam Nabarz Copyright © 2008.

The Copyright of each article is retained by their respective authors.

Published in 2008 by 'Web of Wyrd Press'

An imprint of BECS Ltd.

http://www.webofwyrdpress.com

For mailing list:

http://www.myspace.com/webofwyrdpress

All rights reserved. No part of this book may be reproduced or utilised in any form or by any means, electronic or mechanical, including photocopying, recording, or by any information storage and retrieval system, without permission in writing from the publisher.

Table of Contents

Acknowledgments	4
Editorial.	5
Section 1: academic papers.	7
Factors determining the outside projection of the Mithraic Mysteries by Dr. Israel Campos Méndez	7
The Mithras Liturgy: cult liturgy, religious ritual, or magical theurgy? Some aspects and considerations of the Mithras Liturgy from the Paris Codex and what they may imply for the origin and purpose of this spell by Kim Huggens	23
Section 2: Arts.	52
'For example Mithras' part II exhibition by Farangis Yegane.	52
The Suncircle	52
The Wind	54
Mithras slaying the Bull	57
The Sacrifice in the Abrahamic Religions	60
Lithographs	62
Mithras-Phanes art piece by James Rodriguez	64
Temple of Mithra in Garni, Armenia, photos by Jalil Nozari	65
Mithras artistic depiction by Robert Kavjian	70
Section 3: Religious Articles	71
MITHRAS SOL INVICTUS Invocation by M. Hajduk	71
Ode to Aphrodite by Sappho, translated by Harita Meenee	72
Norooz Phiroze by Farida Bamji	74
Disappearing Shrines by S. David	76
Moving Shrines by S. David	77
The Sleeping Lord by Katherine Sutherland	79
The right handed handshake of the Gods by Payam Nabarz	80
Book Reviews	95
Beck, R. The Religion of the Mithras Cult in the Roman Empire. Mysteries of the Unconquered Sun. Review by: Dr. Israel Campos Méndez.	95
Adverts	98

Acknowledgments

Front cover painting: The Suncircle by Farangis Yegane, from 'For example Mithras' part II exhibition.
Measurements total: 170 x 260cm; diptych; acrylic on canvas.
The Suncircle. The torches held up and down by Cautes and Cautopates marking the rotation of earth and sky. Photo produced here by kind permission of Farangis Yegane.

To Alison Jones for reading of this manuscript and her numerous helpful comments and discussions.

Hear, golden Titan, whose eternal eye
With matchless sight illumines all the sky.
Native, unwearied in diffusing light,
And to all eyes the object of delight:
Lord of the Seasons, beaming light from far,
Sonorous, dancing in thy four-yoked car.

- The Orphic Hymn to the Sun, Translated by Thomas Taylor (1792)
http://www.sacred-texts.com/cla/hoo/hoo12.htm

Editorial.

Mithras Readers: An Academic and Religious Journal of Greek, Roman and Persian Studies is dedicated to all the religions of the classical world. We invite submissions of academic papers from researchers and spiritual articles from practitioners of the religions of the classical world. We also welcome classical world based art work, both modern interpretations and traditional forms.

Occasional articles covering the non-religious aspects of the ancient Greco-Roman or Persian world will be considered, for example dealing with geopolitical, cultural, or relevant military history.

The Journal is divided into three sections. Part 1 contains the academic papers; Part 2 Mithraic based art work, sculptures and paintings; and the Part 3 there are religious articles by modern practitioners, rites, hymns and poetry. Authors should state which section they wish their papers to be included in.

Authors receive one complimentary copy of the issue in which their article appears. All articles featured in the journal remain the Copyright of their authors and artists, and authors are responsible for obtaining Copyright permission for all previously published or Copyrighted materials that are used / included in their submissions.

Materials are to be submitted in English and should not normally exceed 9000 words, and should be presented in 12 point Garamond font.

Materials are to be submitted electronically as .doc or .rtf files, and images should be submitted as JPEG files unless otherwise discussed, and should be provided at the size intended for production at a resolution of 600 dpi. References should be numbered in the text and appear as numbered endnotes at end of the article. Any bibliography should also be located at end of the article.

To contact us or send your submissions please email us at: nabarz@hotmail.com

Payam Nabarz
Editor.

http://www.myspace.com/nabarz

Section 1: academic papers.

Factors determining the outside projection of the Mithraic Mysteries by Dr. Israel Campos Méndez

University of Las Palmas de Gran Canaria, Spain.

Abstract

This paper analyses some of the special features in the social composition of those initiated into the Mithraic mysteries. It also examines how the relationship of the Mithraic Cult with the Roman political power was and how a god of Persian origin could establish this relationship.

In the complex and assorted market represented by the religious scene present in the Greek-Roman world of the last Era, any study of what could be the offer made by any new religion to neophytes in trying to get hold of a share of the mentioned market becomes very interesting. That is particularly true if we attend to the fact that these new religions had beaten the initial barriers to entry into society and obstacles long established by the Roman local authorities on the religious practices that came from the East.

Regardless of whether the general parameters of the religiousness had changed during the Greek period or not, we want to focus on the main characteristics of Mithraic Cult in order to study in-depth what an individual could find at this time of new religious offerings. Together with the salvation and eternal life promises inherent to other mystery practices developed in the East, it should be also recognized that a strong psychological component contained in the group of ritual practices developed in a communal environment. The eschatological promises potentially offered by any worship related to Mithra take place in the course of a social experience, in which the individual initiated into the worship creates membership links to another group different from the family, the tribe, the *Urbs* or the State. The Mithraic experience is a communal experience in which the *mystes* finds a new home, new people and a new identity. The celebrations and ceremonies performed in the 'mithraeum' were organised to strengthen each initiated's hope, and, to provide the individual with a full sense for his daily life. In fact, regardless of the soteriologic offer, it can be assumed that most of the individuals initiated into these mystery worships were just hoping to satisfy many of their non-spiritual needs, such as security, a social network, protection, etc.(1)

The literature has traditionally accepted the statement made by F. Cumont (1967, 132) about the fact that the large variety in the social backgrounds of the followers of the god Mithra, and, supposedly, the subsequent level of 'democratization' was one of the factors that could have boosted the membership of the mentioned cult. The presence of members of each social hierarchy among the different initiation degrees that exist in the Mithraic cult, from slaves to emperors, has been used to prove, on one hand, the significant degree of establishment acceptance that, somtimes, characterized the cult of Mithra; and, on the other hand, has motivated the proposal of the image of the *mithraeum* as a meeting point for Roman society. However, among the scholars who have devoted an special interest to study the social aspects of Mithraism, there is some scepticism about any kind of generalization related to the social composition, or the assumption of the equality between the represented groups(2). In fact, although it turns out to be highly difficult to know how established the internal relationships were between the members of a Mithraic community, it is obvious that there were different levels of vertical and horizontal interrelationships. They were defined taking into account the origin and even each individual's personal ability, in the same way that it was necessary for the figure of a sponsor (*mystagogus*) who would act as introductory person of each neophyte in the worship. With these determining factors, there were mechanisms assigned to monitor, at least in a general way, the social relationships established within the community of believers were clarified.

Mithraism, as R. L. Gordon (1971, 92-121)(3) says, was used in the Roman army as an instrument that empowered the hierarchical structure of the legions and the spirit of discipline and sacrifice common in the military life. It should be emphasized how important a role that many *mithraea* camps along the *Limes* could have played in the lifes of Roman Legion officers, who had a special prominence not only in the introduction of the cult, but also subsequently in the highest ranks of the initiation scale. We should also take into account several factors that may clarify the egalitarian image people have regarding the obtaining of the different ranks. It is known that a strong stratification characterises the Mithraic community (4), where each body and each individual has a very specific role within the liturgy, and where there is a general distinction between ranks playing a servant role ('ὑπηρετουτντες') and ranks acting as participants ('μετέχοντες')(5). This makes us speculate that some sort of discrimination regarding the obtaining of the higher ranks had to exist, so that these ranks were reserved for the individuals that had a proven status within the social system of each mystery cell. The cultural levels were presented as another distinguishing factor, since the philosophical and esoteric components in the Mithraic theology required some training rank that made it unachievable for illiterates, or for the inexperienced. Another criteria could have derived from the right of the president of the community to decide who could enter the initiation process and who could make progress through it. The leader could set the social standard and the numerical composition of each *mithraeum*; therefore, in order not to jeopardize his initiation progress any individual should have enough prestige and training (6). This last criterion would probably have been found in direct relation with the space reality determining the physical place used for the Mithraic cult. In general, the reduced size of the *mithraea* do not allow for the existence of communities that have achieved a particularly large number of members. Even in the case, as Volken (2003) has stated, that two Mithraic groups shared a single temple, it is logical to consider that any increase in the size of the the communities was conditioned by the need of adapting themselves to the place where their religious ceremonies were held.

The epigraphic testimony is a basic element in any attempt of approach to the social composition of the Mithraic communities. Through these documents, mainly collected in the compilations of Cumont (1896, 1899) and Vermaseren (1956, 1960)(7), we know that the initiated into the different Mithraic ranks made a public confession of their belonging to this brotherhood, including it as a distinguishing characteristic or element of their *cursus honorum*. The social composition of the initiated is structured by slaves, slaves that have succeeded in reaching the freedom, merchants, knights, senators, and, even some emperors. This means that in several cases, the criterion of being a

Roman citizen was not the common characteristic shared by these people, but instead their attraction to the personality of the god Mithra. The prominence represented by individuals of eastern origin in several communities (possibly Greek-speakers of Asian origin related to Asia Minor and Armenia) allowed these people to hold the higher ranks (Court 2001, 186) during some periods in these communities.

A singular aspect shown by the Mithraic cult, as compared to the other mystery religions that flourished in Rome during this period, is its attitude regarding the women; a circumstance whose origins are not explained within the Greek-Roman context. In this sense, we have proposed that such an specificity usually corresponds to a reminiscence left by the characteristics of the worship of Mithra within the Iranian context. More information can be found in in my study (Campos 2006a, 5-22).

As opposed to the other mystery religions, that since their beginnings within the frontiers of the Empire had carried out a set of practices and processions(8) that allowed a link to the citizenship with it (both the initiated and the uninitiated citizenship), the Mithraic religion always declined any sort of public ceremony. In fact, the *mithraeum* had a particular architectural structure that prevented outsiders from watching what happened in the main chamber. It is likely that this situation strengthened the brotherhood links and the secrecy held in each community, while simultaneously sanctioning – from an outsider's perspective -- the spirit of alternative worship opposed to the traditional religious habits. At the beginning, this alternative nature was present in all of the Oriental cults, but the State progressively assumed (directly or indirectly) influence on it and was always alert to prevent any movement that could cause doubt in the ruling social and political status quo. Although the exotic and individualizing character survived, all these alternative religious forms were 'tamed' by the general interests of the Roman power (Alvar 1991, 82-83; Beck 2006, 175-196).

This situation leads us directly to analyse the relationship between the Mithraic worship and the Roman political power. The first mention made about Mithra related with a Roman emperor is the one (Dio Casio, 62.1.7.) in which Nero is identified by Tiridates as a reincarnation of the Iranian Mithra: *I, the descendant from Arsaces, brother of the kings Vologeses and Pacores, am your slave. I have come before you, my god, kneeling down before you as I do before Mithra, in order to make everything you order me; because you are my fate and my fortune.*

It is not possible to describe in detail these mystery elements, or to identify a particular relationship between this emperor and the god (Campos 2006b, 233-4; Beck 1998, 115-128). The worship of Mithra never enjoyed official recognition by the Roman emperors; in spite of the fact that some of them were initiated into thepractices (for example, this is the case of Commodus, cfr. Lampridius, *Hist. Aug., Comm.* 9), or other emperors allowing the creation of mithraea in imperial places (Septimus Severus and Caracalla), or despite the presence of Mithra in official documents such as a monetary issue by Gordian III in the city of Tarsus(9), or despite of the inscription made in *Carnuntum* by the emperors, calling him 'fautor imperii sui' (*CIMRM*, 1698 = *CIL* III, 4413) . Although this is not the appropriate moment to explain this question, it should be pointed out that the references to *Sol Invictus*, that are so frequent in Late Empire emperors' pleas, had not neccesarily an specific relationship with the worship to Mithra(10). Furthermore, many of these emperors did little study of Mithraism, motivated in most cases by the spirit of syncretism that predominated during the III century AD,particulary around the solar worship and that led to the essay of Elagabalus. Similarly, the emperors were conscious of the preminence of Mithraism over the soldiers. Hence, some dedications or performances aligned toMithraism were carried out to ensure the support of some legions, such as the previous mentioned restauration of the *mithraeum* of *Carnuntum* and the reference to Mithra as 'defender of the Power'.

The contrast between the ecumenical Oriental Mithra and the Mithra accessible to identification by everyone has stood out against the hidden and restricted Occidental mystery of Mithra. Our explanation of this situation is based on the fact that the link between Mithra and his Persian origin was present in the Roman conscience. Since the first literary mention in the Roman context, a passage from the poet Statius(11), it is clear the knowledge that the Roman people had about the birthplace of this divinity. Celsus (*Ale. Log.* 72) directly associates the Persian people with the mystery practice (*the Persian people represent the same idea in the Mithras mysteries*), and the same is assumed by Origen when referring to the piece of work of this author: *Celsus, moreover, describes some Persian mysteries, where he says: these truths are obscurely represented by the teaching of the Persian people, whose origin is Persian.* This means that, when referring to this god, it was immediately acknowledged his relationship with the country that, since the defeat of *Carrae* in 53 BC, had become the enemy 'par excellence' of the Roman people (replacing the Carthaginians). The fact that the Empire or the emperor himself publicly stated his affiliation or identification with Mithra, implied some kind of recognition of superiority by the traditional enemy (Turcan 2001, 137-148). From the side of the political power, it must be considered that there was a generalized anti-Persian feeling within the citizens. This hostile feeling is used by a Christian author, Firmicus Maternus (*De err. Prof.* 5,2) to reprimaned the Roman followers to Mithra, for they are putting their faith into an enemy god: *So, what do you respect? In his temples (you can see) rigorously (the liturgy) of the magicians according to the Persian rite, why do you praise the Persian people only in their practices? If you consider yourself worthy of your Roman name, what do you do serving so the Persian liturgies, the Persian laws…?*

This perception is not so surprising if we consider that the worship tof Mithra in the eastern context is an external demonstration through an iconography that linked the god directly to the Arsacid and Sassanid monarchy (12). In this way we find the presence of Mithra in theophoric names of many kings, his image is depicted in the coins and his presence is even more noteworthy in the Taq-i-Rustam relief that commemorates the victory of the Sassanid king Shapur II(13) against the emperor Valerian (AD 260).

The reproach of Firmicus Maternus of Mithra followers is believed to be dated in the first half of the IV century AD. The main point of his criticism derives from the Persian origin of the practiced religion, even though it had been introduced almost three centuries ago within the Roman frontiers andbecame strongly westernised. Therefore, this reality was always present in the minds of a large number of Roman citizensfor number of centries. Jerome (*Adv. Iov*, 2,14) mentions the of work of Eubolos, the neoplatonic philosopher of the II century A.D.

who wrote a treatise about the history of this god, where he referred to the magician roles in the Persian worship of Mithra. So, it is not strange that the mission carried out by the Roman General Stilicho to the Shapur III court at the end of the IV century A.D. was described by the Roman poet Claudian (*De Cons. Stil.* 1,58) in the following way: *The peace is sworn at altars sweet with the fragrance of incense and the harvests of Saba. Fire is brought forth from the innermost sanctuary and the Magi sacrifice heifers according to the Chaldean ritual. The king himself dips the jewelled bowl of sacrifice and swears by the mysteries of Bel and by Mithras who guides the errant stars of heaven.*

There is no information about a mystery practice related to Mithra in this context, so we can assume that the Latin author could have resorted to the term 'mystery' (lat. *secreta*) as a synonym of religion or cult. In fact, the role that Mithra seems to be playing in this scene is the one that, traditionally, was mainly linked to this god through his whole history within the Iranian populations. Since his origin, this divinity represented the embodiment of the idea of contract, and played a leading role in the establishment of political agreements and treaties .

The awareness of his Persian origin was still obvious in spite of the Oriental elements that could be detected within the Mithraic mystery, whose eastern nature was easily identified in the liturgy. This mainly refers to a group of words and iconographic elements that appear in Mithraic contexts and whose Persian origin cannot be hidden. Some of these words were included into the mystery practice, maintaining a Persian origin even though they could have lost their original meaning for the initiated. It is important to understand that these uttered expressions, being Iranian words, did not have validity outside the mystery context in which they were used. For that reason, the use of this terminology conferred a particular character to the Mithraic religion as compared to the other mystery worships. Among the different expressions that appear in the inscriptions and graphites we find *nama*, *nabarzes* (*CIMRM* I 54, 58-61, 67, 823), the names of the assistants of Mithra, *Cautes* and *Cautopates*, and the origin of the word *Arimanius* (*CIMRM* I, 221-222, 369, 833-834; *CIMRM* II, 1773, 1775), linked to the *leontocephalus* (lion head) figure. In fact, Lactancius Placidus, in his comment to the Statius' Thebaid (*Comm. in Stat. Theb.* 1,719-20), makes an explicit reference to the Persian origin of the Mithraic rites; and Nonnus of Panopolis, at the beginning of the V century (*Dionysiaca*. 21,248-9), marked the Iranian region of Bactria as the birthplace of Mithra. However, this did not mean initially a negative attitude by the Roman authorities, something that happened, for example, with the proclamation of prosecution against the Manichaeism enacted between AD 297 and 303 by Diocletian under the accusation of transmitting: *the damnable customs and laws of the Persian people (…) our enemy in this part of the world.*

The self control exhibited by the Roman authorities regarding the categorical condemnation or the public acceptance of Mithraism was conditioned, in our opinion, by the perception of the fact that these mysteries did not imply any kind of danger for the social-political stability of the Empire; and, at the same time, by the need for showing publicly before its population a sense of independency against the enemy 'par excellence'. The wide variety of testimonies that points out the existing knowledge regarding the Persian origin of this divinity states, depending on its context, the intention of using this matter as simple informative data or as a hostility element. However, it seems that what generally prevailed was the assurance that, regardless of his Persian origin and the continuity of a meaningful role in the religious pantheon of the Persian enemy, the mystery category of worship to Mithra did not play an idea-transmission role that could jeopardize the political, social and religious order of the Roman Empire. This situation definitely contributed to the fact that the social relationship networks established within the Mithraic communities did not mean at any time a subversion of the order reached as a consensus by the whole Greek-Roman society of that time.

Dr. Israel Campos Méndez
Facultad de Geografía e Historia
Universidad de Las Palmas de Gran Canaria
c/ Pérez del Toro, 1, 35002 – Las Palmas de G.C.
Spain
e-mail: icampos@dch.ulpgc.es

Short biography

Dr. Israel Campos Méndez is an Assistant Professor in Ancient History at the University of Las Palmas of Gran Canaria (Canary Islands, Spain). His lines of research are related to History of Religion, and in particular to the Cult of Mithra in Ancient Iran and Roman Empire. His Ph. D. was entitled: 'The God Mithra: Analysis of the processes of adjustment of his worship from the social, political and religious frame of the Ancient Iran to that of the Roman Empire'. He has written two books in Spanish about the cult of Mithra in Ancient Persia, and many others papers and articles about Zoroastrian Religion and the Mithraic Mysteries.

ABBREVIATIONS:

CIMRN: - Vermaseren, M.J. 1956: *Corpus inscriptionum et monumentorum religionis mithriacae*, vol. I. (Leiden: Brill Publ.)

- Vermaseren, M.J. 1960: *Corpus inscriptionum et monumentorum religionis mithriacae*, vol. II. (Leiden: Brill Publ.).

SOURCES:

- Alvar, J. 2001: *Los Misterios: religiones "orientales" en el Imperio Romano*. (Barcelona: Ed. Crítica).
- Azarpay, G. 1982: 'The Role of Mithra in the investitures and triumph of Sapur II' *Iranica Antiqua* XVII: 181-191
- Beck, R. 1998: 'The Mysteries of Mithras: a new account of their genesis', *Journal of Roman Studies* 88, 115-128.
- Beck, R. 2006: 'On Becoming a Mithraist: New Evidence for the Propagation of the Mysteries' In Vaage, L. (ed). *Religious Rivalries in the Early Roman Empire and the Rise of Christianity*. (Waterloo: Wilfrid Laurier University Press), 175-196.
- Beck, R. 2006: 'The religious market of the Roman empire: How well does Rodney Stark's model accommodate Christianity's pagan competitors,' in L. Vaage. (ed) *Religious Rivalries in the Early Roman Empire and the Rise of Christianity*. (Waterloo, Ont.: Wilfrid Laurier University Press), 233-252
- Campos, I. 2002: *El culto del dios Mithra en la Persia Antigua*. (Las Palmas de G.C.: ULPGC).
- Campos, I. 2006a: 'Continuity and Change in the Cult of Mithra' *Mithras Reader - An academic and religious journal of Greek, Roman, and Persian Studies*. Vol. 1, 5-22
- Campos, I. 2006b: *El dios Mitra. Los orígenes de su culto anterior al*

Mitraísmo romano. (Las Palmas de G.C.: ULPGC)

- Clauss, M. 1992: *Cultores Mithrae. Die Anhängerschaft des Mithra-Kultes.* (Stuttgart: F. Steiner Verlag)

- Court, M. 2001: 'Mithraism among the Mysteries' in D. Cohnsherbok & M. Court (eds.). *Religious diversity in the Graeco-Roman World: a survey of recent scholarship.* (Sheffield: Continuum International Publishing Group), 182-195

- Cumont, F. 1896 : *Textes et monuments figurés relatifs aux mystères de Mithra.* Vol I. (Brussels: H. Lammertin)

- Cumont, F. 1899 : *Textes et monuments figurés relatifs aux mystères de Mithra.* Vol. II. (Brussels: H. Lammertin)

- Cumont, F. 1967: *Oriental Religions in Roman Paganism.* (London: Dover Press)

- Gordon, R.L. 1971: 'Mithraism in Roman Society: social factors in the explanation of Religious change on the Roman Empire', *Religion* 2, 92-121.

- Gordon, R. 2001: 'Ritual and Hierarchy in the Mysteries of Mithra' *ARYS* 4, 244-274.

- Griffith, A. 1993: *The Archaeological Evidence for Mithraism in Imperial Rome*, PhD diss., Michigan,

- Griffith, A. 2000: '"Mithraism in the private and public lives of 4th-c. Senators in Rome' (online) *Electronic Journal of Mithraic Studies.* Vol. I.: [http://www.uhu.es/ejms/papers.htm].

- Halsberghe, G.H. 1974: *The Cult of Sol Invictus.* (Leiden: Brill Publ.), 117-122.

- Helgeland, J. 1996: 'Roman Army Religion' *ANRW* II, 16.2, 1480-98.

- Laechuli,S. 1967: 'Mithraic Dualism', idem (ed.), *Mithraism in*

Ostia; mystery religion and Christianity in the ancient port of Rome. (Evanston: Northwestern University Press), 44-66

- Laeuchli, S. 1968: 'Urban Mithraism' *The Biblical Archaeologist* Vol. 31,3. Sep., 73-99.

- Mac Dowall, D.V. 1979: 'Sol Invictus & Mithra. Some evidence from the Mint of Rome', In Bianchi, U. (ed.). *Mysteria Mithrae.* (Roma: Brill Publ.), 559-571.

- Nicholson, O. (1983). 'Taq-I Bostan, Mithra and Julian the Apostate: an irony' *Iranica Antiqua* XVIII: 177-179.

- Phythian-Adams, W.J. 1912: 'The Problem of the Mithraic Grades' *JRS* 2, 53-64.

- Rubio, R. 1995: 'La iniciación mitraica y la supuesta subversión del orden social', at Alvar, J. et alii (eds.) *Ritual y Conciencia Cívica.* (Madrid: Ed. Clasicas) 215-225.

- Shapur Shahbazi, A. 1985: 'Studies in Sasanian Prosopography II. The relief of Ardaser II at Taq-I Bustan' *AMI*, 18, 181-185

- Simon, M. 1979 : 'Mithra et les Empereurs', In Bianchi U. (ed.). *Mysteria Mithrae.* (Roma: Brill Publ.), 411-428.

- Soudavar, A. 2003: *The Aura of the Kings. Legitamacy and Divine Sanction in Iranian Kingship.* (Costa Mesa: Mazda Publ.)

- Turcan, R. 2001 : 'Comment adore-t-on un dieu de l'ennemi?' *Topoi. Orient-Occident* 11.1, 137-148

- Volken, M. 2003: 'The development of the cult of Mithra in the Western Roman Empire: a socio-archaeological perspective' (online) *Electronic Journal of Mithraic Studies* vol. III: [http://www.uhu.es/ejms/papers.htm]

Notes

(1) S. Laechuli summarizes it clearly with these words: *the merchants and*

slaves continued their business happily, after finding communal and psychological satisfaction. It was the genius of this urbanized Romanized Mithraism to offer man a new life by leaving him right where he was. Laechuli 1967, 64; in line with this topic and studying in depth a bit more in the implications of the relationships made within the *mithraeum* we recommend the survey of Volken, (online), Beck 2006, 233-252

(2) Among the most significant studies, we must point out the book of Clauss (1992), where a systematic compilation of all the testimonies of Mithra followers checked through the epigraphy is carried out. The work of Griffith (1993) is also so enlightening, as well as her subsequent article, Griffith (2000).

(3) Also Helgeland 1996, 1497-8.

(4) The incorporation and participation into the Mithraic mysteries is done depending on an internal structure set out in a seven-rank scale that the initiated obtains progressively. The evidence from St. Jerome (*Epistola* CVII, 2) about the initiation hierarchy is proved by the information extracted from the epigraphic inscription and by the Mithraic iconography. Other evidences from classic authors about this subject: Cosmas of Jerusalem, *Scholia in Greg. Naz. Carm.*, 102.

(5) Phythian-Adams 1912, 53-64. Together with these initiation ranks, it has appeared in the inscriptions another set of Mithraic designations that could set any kind of organization within some ranks: *stéréôtes, sophistês, syndexios, petitôr, melloléôn, antípater.* We can find a most recent sight to the meaning of the ranks in the context of the Mithraic practices at Gordon 2001, 244-274.

(6) To expand these questions, we can look at the article from Rubio 1995, 215-225; Laeuchli 1968, 73-99.

(7) There is at the moment a project managed by R. Gordon in the electronic publication *Electronic Journal of Mithraic Studies*, with the aim of producing two supplements to the *CIMRM*, that update the

(8) *Certainly, there are no beautiful external rites left in its mysteries.* Celsus, *Ale. Log.* 34.

(9) Mac Dowall (1979, 559-571) studies the lack of reference to Mithra in the Roman mint, pointing out the contradiction between the public role of Mithra in the East and his privacity in the West.

(10) Halsberghe 1974, 117-122. The Mithraic inscriptions showed the following sort: *Sol Invictus Mithra. CIMRM* I,406, 708; II, 315. Simon (1979, 411-428) questions these identifications, clarifying the indiscreet remarks of Cumont and Bidez when giving excessive importance to the testimonies about the relationships between emperors and the Mithraism.

(11) The first reliable testimony that we know in order to recognize the presence of the worship to Mithra within the frontiers of the Empire appears in the piece of work of a Roman poet, P. Papinius Statius, entitled the *Thebaid*, written at the end of the Ist century AD. The two verses that concern us say: 'See who, underneath the rocks of the Persian hole, bends the horns of the unwilling bull'. (I, 719 ss).

(12) In order to know the characteristics of the worship to Mithra in the Persian empire, Campos 2002 and Campos 2006b. About the iconographic testimonies within the context of the Sassanid monarchy, see Soudavar 2003, 107ff.

(13) There exists some controversy around the identification of the Roman emperor represented in this relief: Azarpay 1982, 181-191; Shapur Shahbazi 1985, 181-185; Nicholson, 177-179.

The Mithras Liturgy: cult liturgy, religious ritual, or magical theurgy? Some aspects and considerations of the Mithras Liturgy from the Paris Codex and what they may imply for the origin and purpose of this spell by Kim Huggens

Cardiff University, UK.

I. Introduction

i. *The Mithras Liturgy – history and context*

The *Mithras Liturgy* is part of the fourth century AD 'Greater Paris Codex' of Graeco-Roman magical texts currently residing in the Bibliotheque Nationale, Paris. Having been first published in translation in 1888 by Charles Wessely, it is now part of *The Greek Magical Papyri in Translation* [1] edited by Hans Dieter Betz, and is notable for the fact that it is the only spell contained within the text to have been given a title in the absence of one by the translators. Whereas a few spells (though definitely the minority) have titles such as "Oracle of Sarapis" [2] these titles are original; the title of the Mithras Liturgy was originally unnamed. It was eventually given this name due to its content – a theurgical rite in which the magician aims to achieve union and knowledge of Mithras in his form as a sun god. Translators and commentators were struck by the use of the god Mithras, and concluded that the spell was a liturgy of the Roman cult of Mithras, subsequently naming it "The Mithras Liturgy". [3] From then on commentators took the appellation for granted, and used

---
[1] This text will from now on be abbreviated to *PGM* in the essay and footnotes.
[2] *PGM V.1-53.*
[3] This trend began in 1903 when A. Dieterich published the text with a commentary as *Eine Mithrasliturgie,* in which he said the ritual was a liturgy of the cult of Mithras, slightly adapted by an Egyptian magician.

the spell to draw conclusions about the cult and its structure, rituals, and beliefs. For instance, Harold R. Willoughby writes in *Pagan Regeneration: A Study of Mystery Initiations in the Graeco-Roman World* that:

"If additional evidence is needed [for the death-rebirth focus of the cult of Mithras], *it is found in the fragments of what was probably in its original state a Mithraic liturgy now preserved in an Egyptian magical papyrus dating from about A.D. 300. Professor Albrecht Dieterich, who published this as* Eine Mithrasliturgie, *is of the opinion that the liturgical parts, which consist of invocations, go back to a Mithraic ritual of the final grade of initiation in use perhaps as early is the first century."*

However recent scholarship has rejected the claim that the Mithras Liturgy is a ritual of the cult of Mithras, and the idea is now a contested one. In this article I aim to examine many of the features of both the cult of Mithras and the Mithras liturgy, in order to find any similarities or differences (particularly in philosophy and iconography) between the two. By doing so I hope to come to a conclusion as to whether or not the so-called "Mithras Liturgy" is a ritual of the cult itself, and if it is not I wish to highlight some aspects of both which may hint at common sources and foundations.

It must be borne in mind that the Mithras Liturgy is part of one magician's magical handbook, a handbook that is highly syncretistic and eclectic in nature, which pulls together a vast variety of magical techniques, god names, and mythologies. The collection of texts that forms the handbook appears to be focussed on planetary magic, and it has been suggested that the Great Paris Codex is organized into a solar/lunar division of its spells, [4] with the Mithras Liturgy placed firmly in the 'solar' section. This is because the moon is notably absent from the spell, and this absence is prescribed as a ritual preparation for the spell itself – it must be performed *"…when the moon is invisible."* [5]

The syncretistic nature of the Great Paris Codex means that the Mithras Liturgy is also eclectic, containing many ideas that are not Roman, such as Egyptian, Judaeo-Christian, and Greek terms and concepts. [6] This syncretism is the first stumbling block for a direct categorization of the Mithras Liturgy as a ritual of the cult of Mithras – something we shall examine later.

ii. The Cult of Mithras – history, mystery, and sources

Until recently the main source for our knowledge of the cult of Mithras was the writings of Franz Cumont. [7] However, interest in the cult has piqued in recent decades, so more commentators are writing about it and putting forward new theories. The most important of these is perhaps the re-evaluation of the origins of the cult: once thought to have come from Persia, the proofs for this theory have since been the subject of much scholarly debate and have been disproved. [8] It is generally

---

[4] See Radcliffe G. Edmonds III, *At the Seizure of the Moon – the absence of the moon in the Mithras Liturgy*.
[5] *PGM IV.754*.
[6] For instance, Psyche (Greek) is called upon in *PGM IV.475;* Egyptian ideas of the seven virgins (Hathors) appear in *PGM IV.662;* and a few Christian/Hebrew names for God appear, such as IAO in *PGM IV.592*.
[7] In particular *The Mysteries of Mithra* (first published in 1903), and *The Oriental Religions in Roman Paganism*, (first published in 1911.)
[8] For more on the theory of the cult's Persian origins, and why such origins are not possible, see Manfred Clauss, *The Roman Cult of Mithras,* ch.1. Here Clauss explains the original theory, and shows that although there are similarities between the Persian Mitra and the Roman Mithras, we cannot conclude anything further than

accepted now that the cult of Mithras began in Rome in the 1st century BCE and lasted well into the Christian era, reaching its height in the 3rd and 4th centuries AD. It is clear from the numerous locations of Mithraic temples (called *mithraea* (pl.), *mithraeum* (sing.), or in some cases *spelaeum*) that the cult was widespread [9] and very popular, particularly amongst soldiers. [10]

What we know of the cult has to be gathered from the abundance of surviving mithraea and the images contained within them, because the cult of Mithras was a mystery cult – it kept its rituals and practices largely secret. We do, however, have a couple of accounts of Mithraic beliefs and practices (although many come from Christian writers who may have been sensationalizing their descriptions of the cult), which we can use to confirm the information gathered from the iconography. The lack of texts and the large number of statues, carvings, and mithraeum, means that the challenge we face when studying the cult is one of balance – we must learn to interpret the iconography of the cult, whilst also attempting not to read too much into it.

iii. Explanation of terms

Although a distinction between 'religion' and 'cult' did not exist in Antiquity (except among a few intellectuals), I shall use the term 'cult' to describe the religion of the Mithraists because we today understand what is denoted by the word. The 'cult' of Mithras has certain features it shares

---

the Roman cult of Mithras taking a few ancient Iranian words into their (relatively new) cult.
[9] Mithraea have been discovered in such diverse places as Rome, Heddernheim, London, Ostia, Konjika, Florence, and Tarsus.
[10] This may be due to the fact that one of the seven Mithraic grades was *Miles* – 'Soldier'.

with the other mystery religions contemporary to it that we class as 'cults' (such as the Eleusinian mysteries and the cult of Isis), namely secrecy, initiation rituals, devotion to one or a few linked deities, and often a limitation on prospective initiates and membership. When I use the term 'cult' I do not do so in the same sense as a sociologist might in reference to The Peoples Temple or Aum Shinrikyo, but instead to describe a mystery religion of Late Antiquity.

The term 'theurgy' will be frequently used in this paper, and I shall use it in line with the definition:

"It may be described as magic applied to a religious purpose and resting on a supposed revelation of a religious character." [11]

II. Important Features of the Cult of Mithras – do they appear in the Mithras Liturgy?

If it is the case that the so-called Mithras Liturgy is a ritual of the cult of Mithras as has been claimed by some scholars, we can expect to find some of the cult's defining features in the text, pointing to this origin. A liturgy of a mystery cult will display much of the cult's philosophy and contain its iconography and symbolism – much as the rites of Eleusis seem to have done. [12] As such, what follows is a presentation of some of the cult's features (based largely on iconography and in places a few writings contemporary with the cult), and an examination of the Mithras Liturgy for any appearance of these features.

---

[11] Dodds, E.R. *Theurgy and its Relationship to Neo-Platonism,* p. 61
[12] See Wright, Dudley *The Eleusinian Mysteries and Rites.* The Lesser and Greater Mysteries celebrated by the cult of Persephone and Demeter not only taught the celebrants its philosophy, but also re-enacted its core myths.

i. Planetary Symbolism

The cult of Mithras appears to have divided its membership into seven grades or initiations (more on this in the next section), each one corresponding to a planet (included in the Roman concept of 'planets' are the sun and moon.) We know which planets were associated with each grade because of a series of frescoes found in a mithraeum in Rome (beneath the church of Santa Prisca) that depicted the seven grades and placed the members of each grade under the protection of a planetary god. [13] The mithraeum of Felicissimus at Ostia also adds to these findings with a floor mosaic that depicts iconography of the seven planets in a ladder ascending upwards. The images on this mosaic can also be interpreted as relating to the Mithraic grades. [14]

The lowest grade (Raven, *Corax*), appears to have corresponded to the planet Mercury, followed by the grade of Bridegroom (*Nymphus*[15]) with Venus. Soldier (*Miles*) was associated with Mars, Lion (*Leo*) with Jupiter, Persian (*Perses*) with the Moon, Runner of the Sun (*Heliodromos*) with the Sun, and finally Father (*Pater*) with Saturn. Interestingly, the Sun (which, Mithras being a sun-god, we would expect to find as the highest grade) is

---

[13] Each of these commendations to the planetary gods begins with the greeting 'Nama', of Persian origin. Whilst originally this was thought to prove a Persian origin of the cult, many scholars today believe it was used by the cult to add the authority of an older and more ancient culture, as well as the exoticism that accompanied it.

[14] Image in Clauss, *The Roman Cult of Mithras,* fig.9, p.47.

[15] There was, in earlier scholarship, some dispute over the name of this grade. Franz Cumont, on p. 152 of *The Mysteries of Mithra* says the grade's title is, in the original language, *Cryphius*, or 'Occult', and drew conclusions as to the nature of the grade accordingly. However, as has been demonstrated by Bruce M. Metzger in *St. Jerome's Testimony Concerning the Second Grade of Mithraic Initiation*, this ignores the number of inscriptions that clearly state the second grade as *Nymphus*.

not ruling over the highest grade – instead we find Saturn taking that place.

The focus on planets and the cosmos does not end there in the cult of Mithras. As will be shown later, several mithraeum ceilings are painted to look like a starry night sky, and almost all images of the tauroctony (Mithras slaying the bull) are surrounded by symbols of the seven planetary gods or constellations. [16]

It has already been mentioned that planetary magic seems to be the focus of the Great Paris Codex from which the Mithras Liturgy comes from, but the Mithras Liturgy itself contains what could be seen as the seven planetary gods – the seven "Pole Lords of heaven" [17] and the "7 immortal gods of the world." [18]

It is likely that it is the latter seven figures who represent the planetary gods, since they are invoked or petitioned (in a sequence) in order for the door to the world of the gods to be opened for the magician, and to allow him to petition the sun god Helios. [19] This is tantalizingly similar to the account given by Celsus in Origen's *Contra Celsum*, in which he describes a Mithraic representation of the passage of the soul through the planets: a ladder of seven rungs, each corresponding to a planet and a metal, and at the top of it an eighth gate. [20] Could this be what is

---

[16] This can be seen clearly on, for instance, the bas-relief discovered in London, in the case of the signs of the zodiac, (Cumont, *The Mysteries of Mithra,* p. 122) and on the bas-relief from Bologna in the case of the seven planetary gods (Cumont, *The Mysteries of Mithra,* p. 151.)
[17] PGM IV.676.
[18] PGM IV.620.
[19] PGMIV.620-640.
[20] Origen, *Contra CelsumVI.22*.

described in these lines of the Mithras Liturgy? And could the opening of the door to the world of the gods be this 'eighth gate'? It is certainly possible, however an interpretation of the text as a liturgy of the cult based on the appearance of the seven planetary gods is not a necessity: other possibilities arise, not least that these seven figures do not relate at all to the Mithraic grades, but instead are important in their own right.[21] There is also a possibility that the magician who created this text was familiar with the Mithraic grades and their associated planets, and mixed this (highly potent) symbolism of ascension with a ritual devoted to achieving theurgical ascension.

ii. Seven Grades of Initiation

The seven grades in the cult of Mithras appear to have been designed as a method of ascension in the ranks of membership[22] as well as spiritual ascension. Origen, in *Contra Celsum VI.22* calls the seven grades a "ladder", indicating that each is to be taken on separately and in consequential order. The Emperor Julian also makes mention of spiritual ascension in the Mithraic mysteries:

---

[21] A brief read of the other magical texts collected in the *Greek Magical Papyri* will show that the seven planetary gods are invoked and petitioned without any possible reference to the Mithraic grades – they are viewed as having power in their own rights to grant the magician his wish.

[22] Manfred Clauss suggests however that the named grades were not given to every initiate, but instead to only a few who wished to proceed in the cult in that manner. These members were like priests, whilst those who did not undertake a grade initiation were initiated just the once (into the cult). (See Clauss, *The Roman Cult of Mithras*, p.131-133. This makes sense if we assume the grades are spiritual and mystical in nature: not everybody is interested in spiritual/mystical experience and growth, so not all members of the cult would wish to undertake it. In a similar vein, Cumont suggests that receiving the first three grades did not entitle one to participation in the mysteries, but only to a serving role. (*The Mysteries of Mithra*, p.155.)

"But if I should touch upon that arcane and mystic narration which the Chaldean, agitated by divine fury, poured forth about the seven-rayed god, and through which he leads souls back again to the courts of light, I should speak of things unknown, and indeed vehemently so, to the sordid vulgar, though well known to theurgic and blessed men; and therefore I shall be silent respecting such particulars at present." [23]

However, there is only one text still extant that pays witness to all of the seven grades in the cult of Mithras - St. Jerome's Epistle to Laeta, [24] in which he lists the seven grades in an order that corresponds to the mosaic at Ostia and the frescoes in Rome. [25] Other mentions of the grades serve to support Jerome's account, such as in Porphyry's *De Antro Nympharum 15* where he tells us that the grade of Lion/*Leo* performed its ablutions with honey instead of water (indicating a possible fiery nature of the grade); Tertullian, in *De Corona 15* writes of the grade of Soldier/*Miles*, in which the initiate is offered a crown at sword point at refuses to take it, saying instead "Mithras is my crown".

It is clear that the seven initiatory grades do not directly appear in the Mithras Liturgy. If one wishes to interpret the text they may, however, be found in the aforementioned "7 immortal gods of the world". If this is the case though, it seems strange that a cult which clearly does not advocate passing through every grade overnight (which this ritual would achieve) has as one of its liturgies the Mithras Liturgy. We find in several inscriptions (such as votive offerings) people with titles of the grades,

---

[23] *Oration to the Mother of the Gods* in *Two Orations of the Emperor Julian,* trans. Taylor, Thomas.
[24] Jerome, *Epistle CVII.2*.
[25] Although he also mentions an extra grade that is not found anywhere else – the "Crab", which is in between "Sun" (*Heliodromus*) and "Father" (*Pater*)

such as *Pater* or *Leo* – it would be strange of the members to have a title from one of the lower grades if ascension through all seven immediately was possible. It is also clear that cult rituals were often tied to the initiatory grades, and that members of each grade had a particular function to perform. [26] The Mithras Liturgy completely lacks the symbolism of the seven grades, and is obviously meant to be performed by a solo magician instead of in a group setting. We also know that the cult had different initiation rituals corresponding to each of the grades. [27] This makes it unlikely that the Mithras Liturgy is a ritual of a specific grade.

In regards to the initiatory grades, then, those who support the idea that the Mithras Liturgy is a ritual of the cult need to ask what place it had in the cult. There is nothing to discount the possibility that the cult had other rituals that were not tied to the grades, but it does seem strange that a group who believed the soul ascended via a seven-stepped 'ladder' would have as one of its other rituals the Mithras Liturgy, which by its very nature allows the magician's soul to ascend to the realm of the gods. [28]

---

[26] For instance, it is likely that the Lions of the cult were the incense-offerers during cult rituals: in the Roman mithraeum beneath Santa Prisca the Lions are depicted as offering gifts to the Father, and an inscription reads: *"Receive the incense burners, Father, receive the Lions, Holy One, through whom we offer incense, through whom we ourselves are consumed!"*

[27] Tertullian's description of the crown ritual for the grade of Soldier/*Miles* (*De Corona* 15.3) could be read as an initiation into that grade (it would lose its effect after several repetitions!), as could his description of the honey-purification (*De Antro Nympharum* 15) of the Lion/*Leo* grade (the language is that of instruction in something new and advice for how to continue – appropriate language for initiation.)

[28] *PGM IV.625-629*: *"Then open your eyes, and you will see the doors / open and the world of the gods which is within doors, so that from the pleasure and joy of the sight your spirit runs ahead and ascends."*

It would be easy to reject the idea that the Mithras Liturgy was a ritual of the cult of Mithras based on a view of the seven initiatory grades. We might say that because there were seven grades associated with the seven planetary gods, Mithraism's cosmology split the universe into seven separate spheres through which the soul could ascend individually. [29] These seven spheres certainly do not appear in the Mithras Liturgy, and the magician's soul is not said to pass through seven spheres, doors, or gates. However, I do not think that this supports the conclusion that the Mithras Liturgy is not a cult ritual, because I do not think we can so easily assume a Mithraic sevenfold cosmology – instead the cult is more likely to have held a three-fold cosmology, and to have revered two sun gods. (This is examined in the following two sections.)

iii. Helios and *Mithras – Two Sun Gods?*

Although Mithras was identified with the sun (one of his epithets was "Sol Invictus" – 'the unconquered sun'), Mithraic iconography always depicts Mithras and the sun god (usually Helios or Sol) as distinct and separate figures. [30] Several bas-reliefs show a feast-scene at which both Mithras and Sol (sometimes represented by men from the *Pater* and *Heliodromus* grade) recline on the skin of a flayed bull, [31] in what is

---

[29] This was certainly a view held by Franz Cumont. See *The Mysteries of Mithra,* p.154: *"The seven degrees of initiation through which the mystic was forced to pass in order to acquire perfect wisdom and purity, answered to the seven planetary spheres which the soul was forced to traverse in order to reach the abode of the blessed."* In *Textes et monuments figures,* p.41 he outright rejects a Mithraic origin for the Mithras Liturgy because of this.

[30] See, for instance, the Fiano Romano double-sided relief, in which Sol and Mithras appear clearly as separate entities in separate parts of the image (Clauss, *The Roman Cult of Mithras,* fig.106 p. 148).

[31] Such as the bas-relief of the Mithraic communion found in Konjica, Bosnia (Cumont, *The Mysteries of Mithra* fig.38 p.159); and the Ruckingen double-sided cult-relief (Clauss, *The Roman Cult of Mithras,* fig.71 p.111.)

possibly a ritual reconstruction of the victory meal Mithras and Sol celebrated together before they both ascended in the sun-chariot. [32]

Mithraic images contain several examples of Helios/Sol and Mithras, but interestingly the images of Mithras are strikingly similar to the description of him in the Mithras Liturgy. He is described as:

"... a god immensely great, having a bright appearance, youthful, golden-haired, with a white tunic and a golden crown and trousers, and holding in his right hand a golden / shoulder of a young bull: this is the Bear which moves and turns heaven around, moving upward and downward in accordance with the hour. Then you will see lightning bolts leap from his eyes and stars from his body." [33]

The white tunic can be seen in most images of Mithras, and the golden crown is seen in a Mithraic relief from Roman Nida. [34] The golden shoulder of a young bull may refer to the tauroctony (bull-slaying) seen in nearly all mithraeum, and the description of Mithras as "the bear which moves and turns the heaven around" fits with the idea that Mithras is an 'equinox-pusher' who is outside the universe, as described by David Ulansey. [35] It is uncertain as to whether non-initiates of the cult would be familiar with such imagery, but given that the tauroctony was to be

---

[32] Many reliefs bear a narrative of Mithras and Sol, such as the marble plaque from Alcsut, Hungary currently residing in the Magyar Nemzeti Museum, Budapest; a stele relief from Dacia now in Muzeul de Istorie, Bucharest; and a Romanian cult-relief from Sarmizegetusa now in the Muzeul Banatului, Timisoara. For more on the cult myth of Mithras and Sol, see Beck, Roger, *Ritual, Myth, Doctrine and Initiation in the Mysteries of Mithras: New Evidence from a Cult Vessel*. The Journal of Roman Studies vol. 90 (2000) pp. 145-180.
[33] *PGM IV.695-705.*
[34] In Clauss, *The Roman Cult of Mithras,* fig.14, p.54 and in colour on back cover.
[35] Ulansey, David, *The Origins of the Mithraic Mysteries: Cosmology and Salvation in the Ancient World.*

found in the cult-room (the *crypta* which, due to the nature of mystery cults, it is highly unlikely a non-initiate entered into) on the far wall, [36] it is more likely that such an image was revered as highly sacred and thus kept for initiate's eyes only. This gives us the possibility that the redactor of the Mithras Liturgy was a member of the cult.

David Ulansey concludes from the appearance of both Mithras and Sol that the Mithraists believed in not one but *two* sun gods, and that this is not an original idea at the time of the cult. [37] Ulansey suggests that the Mithraists – like the Middle Platonists and Neoplatonists of the second century AD – saw Sol/Helios as the visible sun and Mithras as the hypercosmic sun located in the *hyperouranios topos* (the place beyond the fixed stars, a realm that is described in Plato's *Phaedrus* [38]). Such a belief in a visible sun and an "intelligible" sun is also found in the theurgical Chaldean Oracles from the second century AD, and written about by Plotinus in the *Ennead*. [39] As such, Ulansey posits a threefold cosmology for the Mithraists (as opposed to a sevenfold cosmology based on the seven initiatory grades) which is best described by Radcliffe G. Edmonds III:

"However, the seven planetary spheres of heaven were not the only cosmological model popular in the Hellenistic and late antique eras. A three-level cosmos – divided into

---

[36] See, for instance, the reconstruction drawing of a mithraeum from Budapest (Clauss, *The Roman Cult of Mithras*, fig.8, p.46). The discovered mithraea tend to share highly similar layouts, indicating that the tauroctony was almost always placed in this place of honour.
[37] See Ulansey, David, *Mithras and the Hypercosmic Sun*. Studies in Mithraism, ed. John R. Hinnells, pp.257-264.
[38] Plato, *Phaedrus,* 246D6-247E6.
[39] Plotinus, *Ennead,* IV.3.11.

a) the material, or earthly, world, b) the ethereal, or cosmic, world, and c) the noetic, or hypercosmic world – is found in a wide range of sources, many of which based their cosmologies upon Platonic ideas that filtered through the Hellenistic world." [40]

In this threefold cosmology, the moon ruled over the lowest realm (earth), and served as a mediator and liminal point between this world and the cosmic and hypercosmic worlds.[41] This possibility of a threefold cosmology as opposed to a sevenfold one seems supported by the fact that in Mithraic iconography the planets, zodiac symbols, and planetary gods tend to be depicted in the same sphere instead of in separate ones.[42]

Although a sevenfold cosmology based on the planetary gods is not present in the Mithras Liturgy, a threefold cosmology based on a Mithraic belief in two suns – the visible, cosmic sun and the intelligible, hypercosmic sun, personified as Sol and Mithras respectively – certainly is. The magician starts the ritual with an elemental invocation and petition, asking the four elements to help him achieve his aim.[43] After this he ascends upwards for the first time in the ritual (out of the lowest realm, the earth), having drawn in breath from the sun's rays,[44] and he is

---

[40] Edmonds, Radcliffe G. *At the Seizure of the Moon*, p 227.
[41] See further, Johnston, Sarah Iles, *Hekate Soteira: A Study of Hekate's Roles in the Chaldean Oracles and Related Literature*, p.29.
[42] See, for instance, the Bononia/Bologna votive-relief (Clauss, *The Roman Cult of Mithras,* fig.52, p.87); and the Barberine tauroctony in which all the zodiac signs are placed in one sphere above the head of Mithras as he kills the bull.
[43] *PGM IV.489-495.*
[44] *PGM IV.540.*

greeted with the appearance of the cosmic realm.[45] Next, the magician sees the fiery doors of the visible, cosmic sun [46] open to reveal the sun god Helios (indicating that the sun god and the sun were viewed in this text in a similar way to how the cult of Ra in Egypt viewed the sun: Ra was not the sun itself, he instead dwelt in the sun. [47]) Only after Helios announces the magician to "the supreme god" [48] are the doors (presumably the doors leading to the hypercosmic realm) opened for Mithras and his retinue to appear. [49] Interestingly, the magician does not ascend through these doors to the place where Mithras descends from, indicating the ritual was not aimed at ascending completely into the hypercosmic realm but to simply achieve revelation from Mithras whilst in the cosmic realm. [50]

---

[45] *PGM IV.545-625.* "…but rather you will see all immortal things. For in that day / and hour you will see the divine order of the skies: the presiding gods rising into heaven, and others setting…"

[46] It is interesting that the magician seems to face some sort of barrier/gateway/door before he ascends to each new level. First, the sun's rays act as a gateway for him to ascend from the sensible realm; secondly he has to "complete the / 7 immortal gods of the world" in order to open the fiery doors through which he can reach the hypercosmic realm. (*PGM IV.620-627.*)

[47] This is demonstrated by the fact that the hieroglyphic figure for the word "sun" is different to that of the name "Ra" and different again from the term "Ra the sun-god". See Allen, *Middle Egyptian: An Introduction to the Language and Culture of Hieroglyphs,* p.29.

[48] *PGM IV.644.*

[49] *PGM IV.660-705.*

[50] One possible explanation for this is that Mithras cannot descend to the lowest realm but only to the cosmic realm. This may be because the moon was often viewed by Neoplatonists, theurgists, and possibly also Mithraists as the gateway through which souls had genesis (descended into the lowest realm), and since Mithras was associated with apogenesis (the soul's ascent out of this realm) and the killing of the lunar bull this would be anathema to him. See Edmonds, *At the Seizure of the Moon,* p.228-232 for Porphyry on the moon as genesis, and the bull as the moon.

From the shared threefold cosmology we can reach a possible conclusion that the Mithras Liturgy was indeed a cult ritual; however another possibility presents itself: that the Mithras Liturgy is a prime example of magical theurgy, and that the cosmology and philosophy of the cult of Mithras shares many features with magical theurgy due to both having similar sources and inspirations. Thus, the remarkable similarities between cult belief and the Mithras Liturgy could be explained as the result of the influence of Neoplatonism and the Chaldean Oracles, with the use of Mithras in the text a mere coincidence. [51]

Sarah Iles Johnston writes of theurgy:

"In theurgy, techniques such as those we encounter in the magical papyri were wed to the cosmological and metaphysical tenets of Platonic philosophy. The theurgist, for example, understood the universe to be divided into the same material and noetic realms that are familiar from the writings of many Middle Platonists and Neoplatonists." [52]

A more detailed study of the Platonic, Middle Platonic and Neoplatonic ideas and how they relate to theurgy is, unfortunately, not in the scope of this paper. [53] However, it is clear that they had an immense influence on

---

[51] He was, after all, a highly popular god, as attested to by the large number of mithraea and the writings of the Emperor Julian, who makes repeated reference to Mithras and the cult, including the festival of the unconquered sun ("sol invictus", the epithet of Mithras). See Emperor Julian, *Oration to the Sovereign Sun* in *Two Orations of the Emperor Julian,* trans. Taylor, Thomas.

[52] Johnston, Sarah Iles, *Riders in the Sky: Cavalier Gods and Theurgic Salvation in the Second Century AD,* pp 303.

[53] For a more detailed study see Johnston, *Riders in the Sky*, Thorndike, *Neoplatonism and its Relation to Astrology and Theurgy,* Shaw, *Theurgy and the*

the metaphysics and practices of theurgy, giving it its defining features: a belief in a threefold cosmology which contains material and noetic (hypercosmic) realms through which the soul can ascend. Finding this same belief in the Mithras Liturgy is not surprising then, since it is certainly an example of theurgy. However, the next section will demonstrate how the Mithraic cult is likely to have been influenced by the same ideas found in Platonism, Middle Platonism, and Neoplatonism, and will ask whether this means the Mithras Liturgy is a cult ritual or if the two just share the same influences.

iv. The Rock Birth, the Mithraeum, Plato's Cave, and the idea of the Soul's Ascension

It is a distinctive feature of the cult of Mithras that the mithraeum discovered are always situated underground, often built beneath another building. In some more rural areas the mithraeum are built into natural caves, whereas in towns and cities this was not possible. Many writers from the first few centuries AD pay attention to this place of worship, often calling it a 'cave'. Porphyry, for instance, writes that:

> *"For according to Eubulus, Zoroaster first of all among the neighbouring mountains of Persia, consecrated a natural cave, florid and watered with fountains, in honour of Mithras the father of all things: a cave in the opinion of Zoroaster being a resemblance of the world fabricated by Mithras… We find too that after Zoroaster it was usual*

Soul: Neoplatonism of Iamblichus and Lewy, *Chaldean Oracles and Theurgy: Mysticism, Magic, and Platonism in the Later Roman Empire.*

with others to perform initiatory rites in caves and dens, whether natural or artificial."
[54]

The ceiling of the temple tends to be vaulted and illuminated by candles or lanterns, giving it the look of the starry sky, [55] and reinforcing Porphyry's comment that the temple was a representation of the "world fabricated by Mithras": it was a microcosm.

It is highly unlikely that people wealthy enough to build and found a mithraeum (although they were often small enough for one man alone to fund) would be unfamiliar with the writings of Plato, especially with the rising popularity of Middle and Neoplatonism during the first two centuries AD. It therefore seems interesting that the underground temple the Mithraists used was distinctly viewed as a cave and a microcosm that could be likened to the cave simile found in Plato's *Republic*, and which is arguably the beginnings of Plato's theory of how a philosopher can raise his 'mind' (though here the soul is also implied) beyond this world to the noetic world through contemplation on the world of True Forms. Given that the Mithraists appear to have worshipped Mithras as a saviour god who could help them ascend out of the sensible world into the noetic realm, [56] the Simile of the Cave from Plato is fitting for the Mithraic cult.

---

[54] Porphyry, *De Antro Nympharum 6*. For other accounts of the worship of Mithras in a cave or cave-like temple, see Tertullian, *De Corona 15*.
[55] See, for instance, the Nida/Heddernheim mithraeum II which has a vaulted, starry ceiling. (Clauss, *The Roman Cult of Mithras*, fig.11, p.50.)
[56] See Porphyry, *De Antro Nympharum 6*. Beck writes: *"it was into a 'mystery' of this double process of the soul's entry and exit that the Mithraists inducted their initiates…"* p.159 *Ritual, Myth, Doctrine and Initiation in the Mysteries of Mithras*.

In the Simile of the Cave, Plato describes this world as a shadowy cave where prisoners are chained, unable to see anything but the shadow puppets being created by their jailors behind them. The prisoners believe the shadows to be truth. However, one prisoner manages to escape and finds his way out of the cave, ascending into the brightly lit world. At first he is blinded by the light of the sun, but after his eyes accustom he realizes the truth. (Note here the emphasis on sun imagery in the analogy.) [57]

Also keeping in mind that we know from Celsus that the seven initiatory grades were seen as a ladder for the soul's ascension, and that the Mithraists believed in two sun gods (visible sun and noetic sun – the sun of Plato's world of True Forms), it seems an undeniable conclusion that the mithraeum's symbolism was geared towards being a microcosm which the initiates (like Mithras) could ascend out of.

The iconography that relates the idea of the soul's ascension as akin with that of Mithras' ascension is the "Rock birth" figures [58] found in many cult temples. [59] In these figures, Mithras is represented as being born from a rock with both arms upraised. It is clear that this rock – like the mithraeum and cave – represents the earth. [60] Most striking is the Barberine tauroctony, which (above the bull-slaying scene) has a rock-

---

[57] Plato, *The Republic,* Book VII.514a-521b.
[58] We also have evidence of Mithras being seen as 'rock-born' from literary sources, such as Justin Martyr. In *Dialogue with Trypho 70* he writes: *"And when those who record the mysteries of Mithras say that he was begotten of a rock, and call the place where those who believe in him are initiated a cave…"*
[59] See, for instance, the St. Clement/Rome bas-relief (Cumont, *Mysteries of Mithra,* fig. 30 p. 130).
[60] See, for instance, Clauss, *The Roman Cult of Mithras,* p.62-70. The snake that is so often depicted curled around the base of the rock represents the earth also.

birth figure not only being born from the rock but also breaking through the sphere of the planets and constellations, and entering a sphere beyond them. (cf. earlier section on a threefold Mithraic cosmology.)

So, Mithras is born from the rock (sensible world), Mithraists are offered rebirth from that same world by participation in the mysteries, and Platonism, Middle Platonism, and Neoplatonism all teach a belief in the soul's rebirth/ascension from the sensible world into the noetic realm. Such an important feature of the cult should appear in the Mithras Liturgy if the Liturgy is a ritual of Mithraism.

But it does not do so directly. Indeed, the only vision of Mithras the magician is given is that of him *descending* from the hypercosmic into the cosmic realm. [61] The iconography of the rock birth is not present in the text. However, the metaphysical and philosophical concept of rebirth from the cosmos are certainly present in the Mithras Liturgy, and are some of its clearest ideas.

The language of the Mithras Liturgy is that of death, birth, and rebirth, [62] particularly *PGM IV.715-725:*

> *"O Lord, while being born again, I am passing away; while growing and having grown, / I am dying; while being born from a life-generating birth, I am passing on, released to death – as you have founded, as you have decreed, and have established the mystery."*

---

[61] *PGM IV.795*: "…and a god descending…"
[62] *PGM IV.500-505* "…give me over to immortal birth"; *PGM IV.645-650* "…and who, since he has been born again from you today…".

Here, not only does the magician speak of being born out of the sensible world into the realm above, he also establishes that Mithras founded the mystery of this act. Although the imagery of the rock birth is not present, the idea of it is.

The Mithras Liturgy is a ritual aimed at ascension out of this 'rock'. It may be that, just as Mithras was born out of the rock of the sensible world, so the magician/initiate is able to do so through this ritual. In the cult of Mithras the rock birth appears to have promised the initiates salvation in the form of ascension, and the same idea appears here in the Mithras Liturgy. However, just like the other features of Mithraism that appear in the Mithras Liturgy, it would be easy to see how – given the Platonic origin of the idea of ascension out of the sensible realm - they merely reflect the shared sources and philosophical bases of the Liturgy and the cult, instead of definitively proving that the Mithras Liturgy belongs to the cult.

v. Community and the Communion Meal

We have already seen how the cult of Mithras had ritual meals during their worship, and how the membership of each mithraeum was divided into grades and priests. [63] These two features point to a communitarian

---

[63] Justin Martyr also attests to ritual feasts in *1 Apology 66:* "*...that Jesus took bread, and when He had given thanks, said, "This do ye in remembrance of Me, this is My body; "and that, after the same manner, having taken the cup and given thanks, He said, "This is My blood; "and gave it to them alone. Which the wicked devils have imitated in the mysteries of Mithras, commanding the same thing to be done. For, that bread and a cup of water are placed with certain incantations in the mystic rites of one who is being initiated; you either know or can learn.*"

aspect of the cult, a social side to it. [64] It is clear that this is one aspect not present in the Mithras Liturgy, and this tells us a lot about the text itself, its purpose and origin: the Mithras Liturgy appears to be a *private*, theurgical practice intended for one magician only. [65] It is most certainly *not* a 'cult ritual' since it involves only one person – and the cult of Mithras' rituals that we know of were group rituals or they involved at least two people (usually the initiator and the initiand.) What is it then?

III. Conclusion – What is the Mithras Liturgy?

Although the Mithras Liturgy does share many of the features of the cult of Mithras, I don't believe this leads us inevitably to the conclusion that it is a cult ritual. It significantly lacks certain cult features, such as the tauroctony, [66] which cannot be explained by simple regional/cultural variations of the cult. Instead, there are three possibilities:

1) That the redactor of the text (the magician) was an initiate of the cult of Mithras, and so was familiar with the philosophy and iconography of the cult. He was a theurgist and wished to achieve a revelation from a divine being (who for him would be Mithras.)

---

[64] Some men may have joined the cult specifically to gain social status, as is the case with other mystery cults.
[65] See *PGM IV. 480-485:* "… so that I alone may ascend into heaven as an inquirer and behold the universe."
[66] Although Edmonds argues that although the tauroctony is not present, the timing for the ritual is appropriate for the bull-slaying: *"The ritual preparations for the Mithras Liturgy, then, are prescribed for the time that is most appropriate to the Mithraic bull-slaying, when Mithras as the power of apogenesis overcomes the power of genesis in the form of the lunar-bull."* p.237 *At the Seizure of the Moon.*

2) That the redactor of the text was *not* an initiate of the cult, but was instead familiar with Platonism, Middle Platonism, and/or Neoplatonism, and these ideas are highly similar to those we find in the cult of Mithras.

A third possibility is that the Mithras Liturgy is a cult ritual. However, it is a very different kind of ritual to any of the other cult rituals, since it is private and not tied to any single grade. The likelihood of it being a cult ritual is lessened by the fact that the "7 immortal gods" would correspond to the grades, but they are 'completed' in one ritual – something it is unlikely the cult would have approved of.

The highly potent and multi-layered symbolism and philosophy of the Mithras Liturgy, as well as the focus on Mithras instead of any other god (and in conjunction with Helios, his usual 'friend' from Mithraic iconography) suggests to me that the first option is more likely. If this is the case, the Mithras Liturgy could tell us a great deal about the philosophical concepts of ascension in the cult of Mithras.

Although a more thorough study of the following possibility would be out of the scope of this paper, I believe the Mithras Liturgy could possibly be a ritual whereby the magician (an initiate of the cult who has already passed through the seven initiatory grades[67]) finally achieves immortality through ascension out of the sensible world-rock by passing

---

[67] In the Mithras Liturgy he says he has been "… sanctified through holy consecrations" (*PGM IV.520.*) Could these holy consecrations be the seven initiatory grades?

through the "eighth gate" spoken about by Celsus in relation to the Mithraic ladder:

"For in the latter there is a representation of the two heavenly revolutions, of the movement, viz., of the fixed stars, and of that which take place among the planets, and of the passage of the soul through these. The representation is of the following nature: There is a ladder with lofty gates, and on the top of it an eighth gate." [68]

He goes on to describe seven gates as corresponding to a planet and a metal, but makes no further mention of the eighth gate except that it leads to the region beyond the fixed stars, and we know the seventh gate is that of the sun. Interestingly, the floor mosaic of Felicissimus, Ostia, [69] that bears an image of a ladder with symbols of the seven grades and planets on it also has an eighth section above the grades. [70]

The magician may have passed through the seven 'gates' in the cult, and now he performs this ritual for his soul to pass through the final gate – the gate leading out of the cosmic world he has just passed through and into the hypercosmic. [71]

Biography

Kim Huggens is a current PhD student in the Ancient History department of Cardiff University, where she also recently completed an

---

[68] Celsus, in Origen *Contra Celsum* 6.22
[69] See Clauss, *The Roman Cult of Mithras,* fig.9, p.47.
[70] See also Ulansey, David, *The Eighth Gate: The Mithraic Lion-Headed Figure and the Platonic World Soul.*
[71] It is interesting to note that the seventh gate on Celsus' ladder is that of the sun, and it is the sun the magician must finally pass through in order to reach the realm where he receives a vision of Mithras.

MA in Religion in Late Antiquity with the Religious and Theological Studies department. Her current research interests focus on the magical practices of the Late Antique period, and the possible influences from earlier Hellenistic, Mesopotamian, and Egyptian practices. She is particularly interested in the use of "voodoo" dolls in these periods, and current research is being undertaken to compare the erotic spells from these periods with their contexts of erotic literature and culture.

Kim is also the co-creator of "Sol Invictus: The God Tarot", a Tarot deck exploring the many male deities and their myths throughout the world. Work is underway for a companion deck, "Pistis Sophia: The Goddess Tarot".

Bibliography

Allen, James P. Middle Egyptian: An Introduction to the Language and Culture of Hieroglyphs. *Cambridge University Press, 2000.*

Beck, R, Ritual, Myth, Doctrine and Initiation in the Mysteries of Mithras: New Information from a Cult Vessel. *The Journal of Roman Studies vol. 90 (2000) pp.145-180.*

Beck, Roger, The Mysteries of Mithras: A New Account of their Genesis *in The Journal of Roman Studies vol. 88, (1998) pp. 115-128.*

Bonner, Campbell, A Note on Method in the Treatment of Magical Inscriptions *in The American Journal of Philology vol. 75, no. 3 (1954) pp. 303-305.*

Bonner, Campbell, Note on the Paris Magical Papyrus *in* <u>Classical Philology</u> *vol.25, no. 2 (April 1930) pp. 180-183.*

Clauss, Manfred, The Roman Cult of Mithras: The God and His Mysteries. *Edinburgh University Press, 2000.*

Cumont, Franz, The Mysteries of Mithra. *Chicago Open Court Publications, 1903.*

Cumont, Franz, The Oriental Religions in Roman Paganism. *Dover, 1956.*

Cumont, Franz, Astrology and Religion Among the Greek and Romans. *Dover, 1960.*

Deiter Betz, Hans, ed. The Greek Magical Papyri in Translation *vol. 1. University of Chicago Press, 1996.*

Dodds, E.R, Pagan and Christian in an Age of Anxiety. *Cambridge University Press, 1965.*

Dodds, E. R. Theurgy and its Relationship to Neo-Platonism. <u>The Journal of Roman Studies</u> *vol. 37, Parts 1 and 2 (1947). pp.55-69.*

Edmonds, Radcliffe G. III, At the Seizure of the Moon: the Absence of the Moon in the Mithras Liturgy *in Noegel S. et al.* <u>Prayer, Magic, and the Stars in the Ancient and Late Antique World</u> *pp.223-239. Pennsylvania State University Press, 2003.*

Emperor Julian, Oration to the Mother of the Gods, *in* Two Orations of the Emperor Julian. *Trans. Taylor, Thomas. Hermetic Publishing Company, 1932.*

Emperor Julian, Oration to the Sovereign Sun, *in* Two Orations of the Emperor Julian. *Trans. Taylor, Thomas. Hermetic Publishing Company, 1932.*

Faraone, Christopher A. and Obbink, Dirk, ed. Magika Hiera: Ancient Greek Magic and Religion. *Oxford University Press, 1997.*

Frothingham, A. L, A New Mithraic Relief from Syria *in American Journal of Archaeology vol. 22, no.1 (Jan-March 1918) pp. 54-62.*

Jerome, The Letters of St. Jerome, *in* The Ante-Nicene Fathers *vol. VI, ed. Roberts A. and Donaldson J. Hendrickson Publishers, 1994.*

Johnston, Sarah Iles, Hekate Soteira: A Study of Hekate's Roles in the Chaldean Oracles and Related Literature. *Scholars Press,1993.*

Johnston, Sarah Iles, Riders in the Sky: Cavalier Gods and Theurgic Salvation in the Second Century AD. *Classical Philology vol. 87, no. 4 (Oct. 1992), pp. 303-321.*

Justin Martyr, Dialogue with Trypho, *in* The Ante-Nicene Fathers *vol. I, ed. Roberts A. and Donaldson J. Hendrickson Publishers, 1994.*

Justin Martyr, First Apology, *in* The Ante-Nicene Fathers *vol. I, ed. Roberts A. and Donaldson J. Hendrickson Publishers, 1994.*

Lewy, Hans, Chaldean Oracles and Theurgy: Mysticism, Magic, and Platonism in the Later Roman Empire. *Études Augustiniennes, 1978.*

Luck, George, Theurgy and Forms of Worship in Neoplatonism *in* Magic in Relation to Philosophy

Merlan, Phillip, Plotinus and Magic *in Isis vol.44, no.4(Dec 1953) pp. 341-348.*

Metzger, Bruce M. St Jerome's Testimony Concerning the Second Grade of Mithraic Initiation. <u>*The American Journal of Philology*</u>, vol. 66, no. 3, (1945). pp. 225-233.

Nock, Arthur, The Genius of Mithraism *in* <u>*The Journal of Roman Studies*</u> vol. 27 Part 1: *Papers presented to Sir Henry Stuart Jones. (1937) pp. 108-113.*

Origen, Contra Celsum, *in* The Ante-Nicene Fathers *vol. IV, ed. Roberts A. and Donaldson J. Hendrickson Publishers, 1994.*

Plato, Phaedrus, *trans. Hackforth R. Cambridge University Press, 1952.*

Plato, The Republic, *trans. Desmond Lee. Penguin Books, 1987.*

Plotinus, The Ennead. *Trans. MacKenna S. and Page B.S. PL Warner, 1917.*

Porphyry, De Antro Nympharum. *Online text at http://www.thedyinggod.com/chaldeanmagi/sources/porphyry.html accessed 1/06/06*

Shaw, Gregory, Theurgy and the Soul: Neoplatonism of Iamblichus. *Penn State University Press, 1995.*

Ulansey, David, Mithras and the Hypercosmic Sun *in Hinnels, John R. ed* <u>*Studies in Mithraism*</u> *pp. 257-264. "L'Erma" di Bretschneider, 1994.*

Ulansey, David, Origins of the Mithraic Mysteries: Cosmology and Salvation in the Ancient World. *Oxford University Press, 1991.*

Ulansey, David, *The Eighth Gate: The Mithraic Lion-Headed Figure and the Platonic World Soul.* Online at http://www.well.com/user/davidu/eighthgate.html accessed 13/01/06.

Willoughby, Harold. R. Pagan Regeneration: A Study of Mystery Initiations in the Graeco-Roman World. *University of Chicago Press, 1929.*

Wright, Dudley, The Eleusinian Mysteries and Rites. *Ibis Press, 2003.*

Section 2: Arts.

Some of the images in this section are shown twice here: in colour and in black and white, so that the readers who are reading the PDF downloadable version of the Journal can see the colour images. The printed version is only black and white and both images appear in black and white.

'For example Mithras' part II exhibition by Farangis Yegane.

Photos and article here are produced her by kind permission of Farangis Yegane. For further information and to see the exhibition in full colour see the website at: http://mithras.two.farangis.de/page3.htm
The Part I of the exhibition was included in Mithras Reader Volume 1 and can also be seen on the website at: http://www.farangis.de/mithras/

Here you get an overview of the works in the series. Part II of 'For Example Mithras' is made up of four acrylic paintings.

The Suncircle

Measurements total: 170 x 260cm; diptych; acrylic on canvas.

The Suncircle. The torches held up and down by Cautes and Cautopates marking the revolvement of earth and sky.

For her exhibition e.g. Mithras, Part II, Farangis tried to separate Mithras - the central figure of the cult - by means of a different way of depiction, from the Roman view and interpretation. Nevertheless, she uses the imagery of the Roman antiquity, especially the sacramental images which depict Mithras slaying the bull, and the sequence of works starts with the figures of Cautes and Cautopates which assist Mithras.

A wide sky and circling suns, as symbols of the visual daily progression of the sun, emphasize the rhythm of light. Holding one torch upwards and one torch downwards, the torch bearers Cautes and Cautopates indicate the direction of the light, and at the same time they allude to the coming into life and light, and to the cessation of life and darkness.

Farangis tries to bring across that a cosmic order does not leave anything to disappear into an eternal darkness, nor does the life-creating brightness incessantly rule our lives.

Farangis connects in this picture, which is primarily dedicated to Cautes and Cautopates, further images that we are familiar with from the Roman Mithras mystery, like for example the raven, the serpent, the dog, the scorpion, and also young Mithras as born from the rock. Very consciously the slaying scene is not shown here, thus no fraction of death is being depicted. An anthem for light and life in a bright colorfulness seeks to touch the viewer.

The Wind

Measurements total: 100 x 360; consists of 5 parts, acrylic on canvas.

The Wind. The wind gods and Mithras rejecting to kill.

With an emphasis on the width of the sky, that we see on the painting consisting of 5 separate parts, Mithras is positioned in the center and to his sides are the four wind-gods. Farangis shows Mithras here with the cosmic symbol elements. He is shown in his coat, that the wind blows open, the inside of the coat is the sky with its stars.

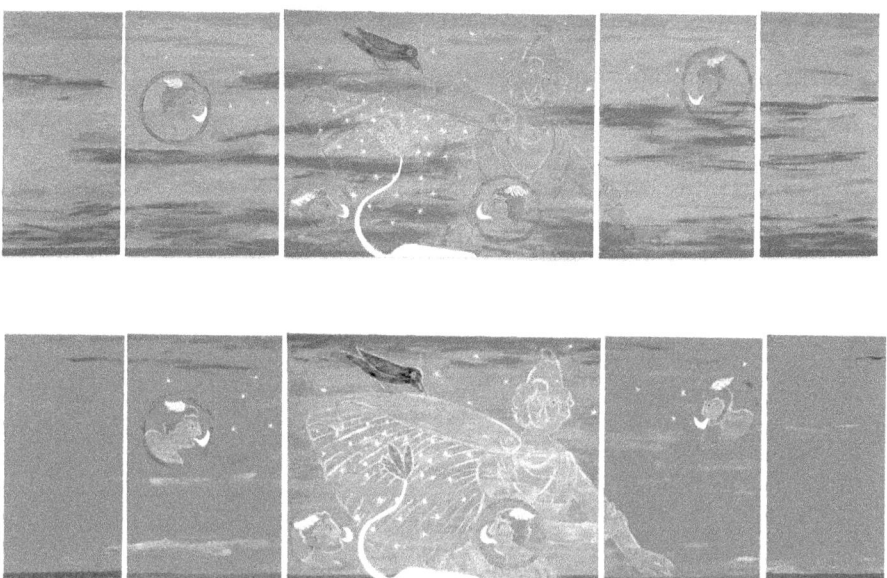

Mithras is sitting on the back of the steer, the steer holds his tail upwards and the tip of the tail is a threefold ear of grain. The tip of the steers tail as a threefold ear of grain is a symbol taken from the old Persian mythology pertaining to the figure of Mithras. Mithras is generally recognizable in the moment in which he takes hold of the steers' head, but with this picture Farangis has painted a position for the slayer that has not been depicted like this before, because here we see Mithras in his decision to refrain from killing the steer. By holding back the hand that wants to kill, he resists to become a murderer by divine command.

In the cosmic piety of the Mithras mysteries the raven plays an important role. The raven is mostly depicted as sitting on the soft coat of Mithras, and facing him directly. Since the dwelling places of birds are both sky and earth, birds often have been attributed a mediating role between the gods of heaven and the earthly world of people.

The four wind gods left and right, high and low, indicate the four wind directions. In many ancient languages wind seen as closely related to breathe, breath and air. In this way, on this picture Mithras has not taken the animals breath, but has preserved life. He has integrated into the cycle of life within a cosmic order and has withheld himself against the divine command to kill.

Mithras slaying the Bull

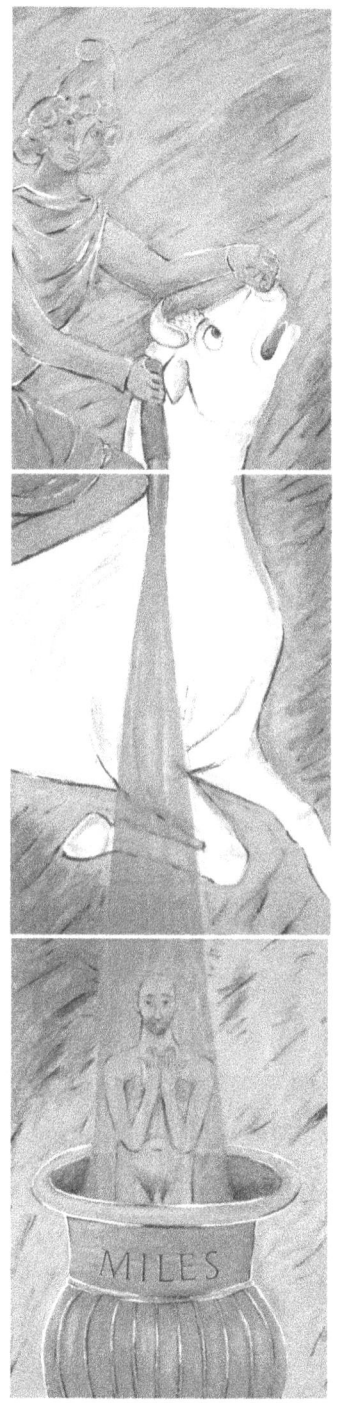
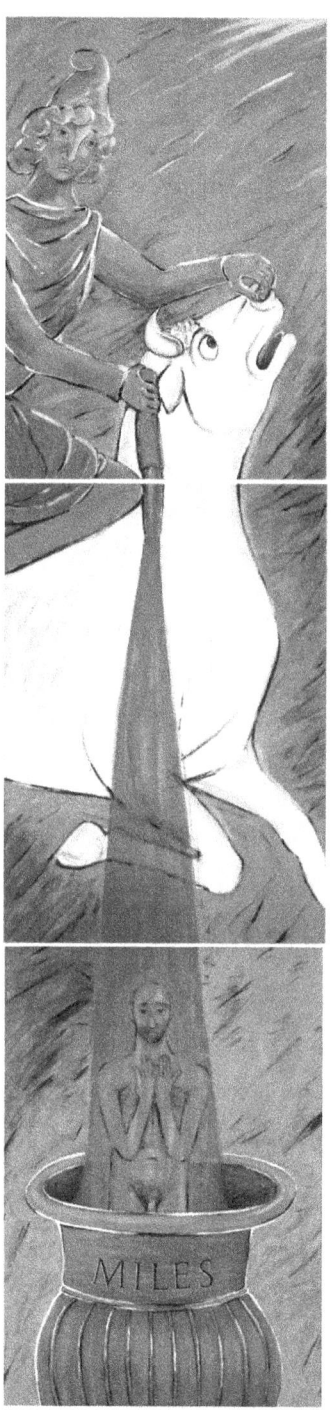

Measurements total: 100 x 420cm; triptych, acrylic on canvas.

The Slaying of the Bull. The sacrifice in the Mithras cult.

This vertical triptych shows us Mithras as him who is slaying the bull. He holds the animal at its hard breathing nostrils to incapacitate the breath. To block any living beings ability to breathe occurs often as a part of killing rituals because the method increases death agony.

In the process of slaughter Mithras pushes his short sword into the carotid artery of the animal and a bloodstream rushes out of the wound into the big clay vessel which Farangis gives the meaning of a baptismal font. In the vessel a naked Miles (Roman soldier) stands immersed in blood. The sacred action takes place at the moment the blood of the sacrificed animal turns into blood that creates life.

To kill living beings as a sacrifice in order to create new life is an act which different religions have been practicing for a very long time. Especially in the monotheistic religions, acts of killing, as a proof of obedience, assure God's favor and promise a redemption from guilt and sin in the sense of a purification.

In this painting Farangis gives an extended view of Mithras, who kills the bull. Images of the scene on the sacramental altars often show Mithras as turning his head away from the animal and looking to an imagined upper point, as if there was something which in a super ordinate way gives an order to kill, and he, Mithras, simply fulfills the deed like an obedient servant.

On this triptych two aspects of the position of one who believes in God are pointed out: to kill a creature when God ordains you to do so, and to appear in front of God as being purified through the shedding the blood of a sacrifice.

The Sacrifice in the Abrahamic Religions

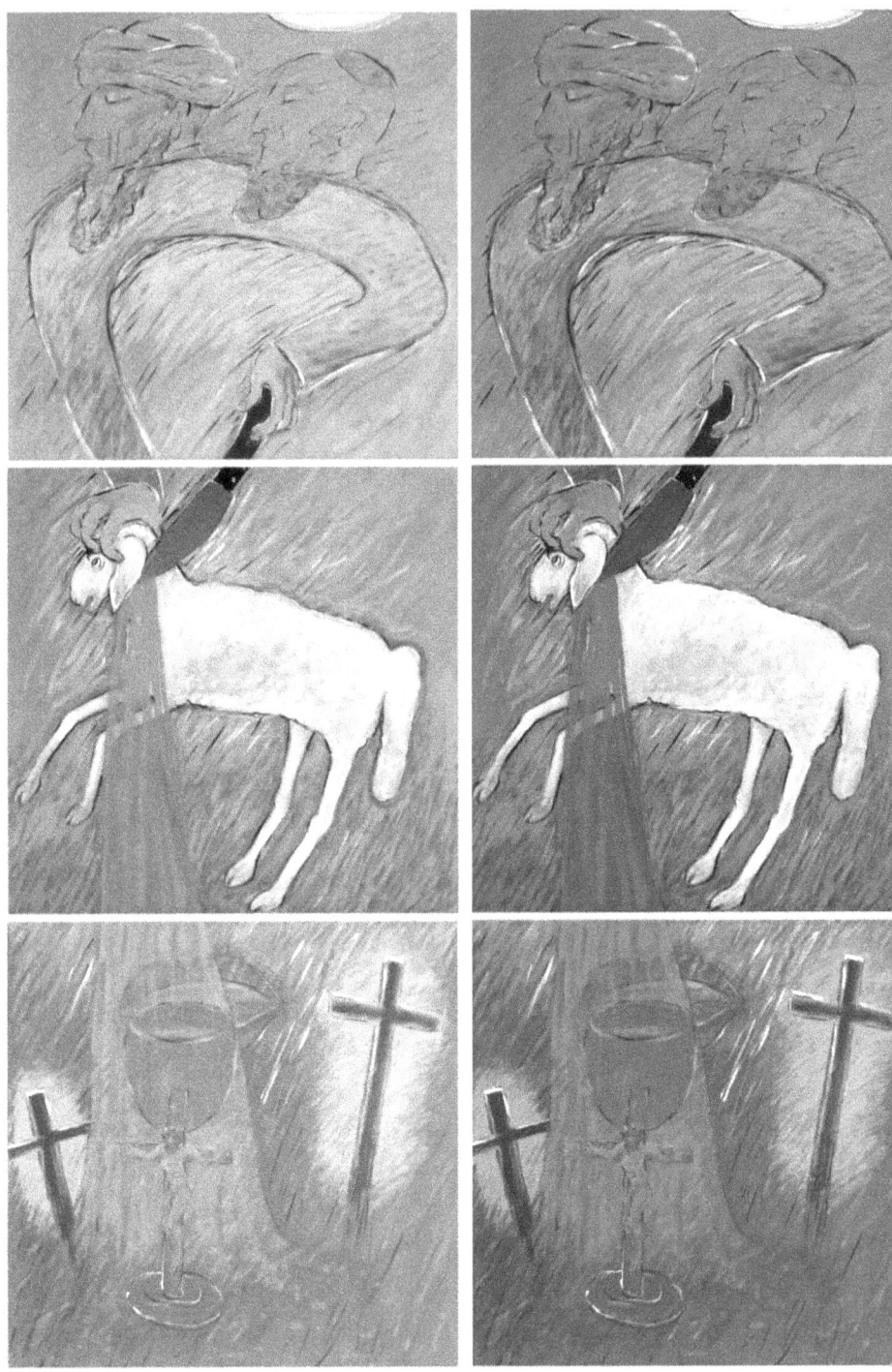

Measurements: 125 x 380; triptych, acrylic on canvas.

The Sacrifice in the Abrahamic Religions. The sacrificed life as a questionable tribute for a contract between man and God.

As an extension of the thought about the sacrifices' death as a necessity for the creation of new life, and the thought about absolute obedience within a belief, we see an example in this big vertical triptych.

Farangis shows an Islamic and a Jewish priest with the same posture, as Mithras, the slayer of the steer, typically displays it; how with his sight turned away he pushes the short sword into the throat of the sacrificed animal and how the animal dies bleeding. Here too, analogous to the bleeding steer of the Mithras mystery, the blood of the sacrificed animal is poured into a vessel - now a large drinking glass. In the depiction of three crosses pertaining to Christian symbolism and with the rough indication of a mouth that wants to drink this blood, a linkage that stands between the Abrahamic religions becomes plain.

In the range of works entitled 'For Example Mithras' Farangis has dealt with a subject which is currently highly sensitive. In the first few years when she started to work on this theme, it was still rare that contemporary western artists dealt critically yet spiritually with the theme religion. This theme was more expected from the arts of so-called native cultures that are still inspired by their archaic gods in their arts. Almost surprised we notice now, that in our search for our lost values and in midst of an extremely tough and painful confrontation with the non-Christian world, more and more often the sense and the nonsense of religiosity is being questioned.

Lithographs

This is an appendix in which we show several additional exhibits of the work series 'For Example Mithras I' by Farangis Yegane.

http://mithras.farangis.de/appendixE.htm
Four colour lithographs (red and black), 38 x 28cm.

Titles:
1. Sol and Mithras,
2. Cult action,
3. The killing of the bull,
4. Rock birth,

Fig. I -II

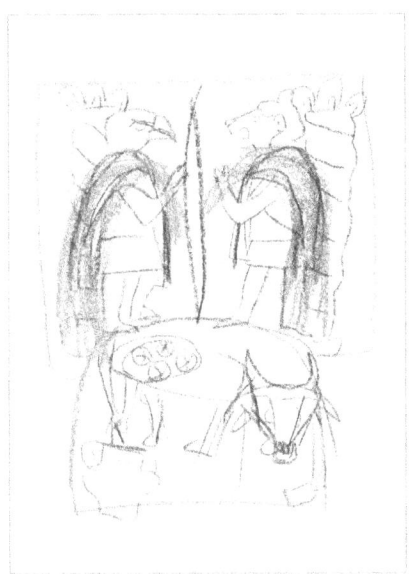

Fig. III-IV

Mithras-Phanes art piece by James Rodriguez

Temple of Mithra in Garni, Armenia, photos by Jalil Nozari

32 kilometres from Yerevan, Armenia, and, at a seven kilometre distance from the famous Monastery of Geghard, lies the Garni compound in which the Mithra temple beautifully overlooks the fortress wall and gates towards the direction of Garni township. The temple's back and sides are to Araz river and valley cliffs.

The building, the best surviving example of its kind globally, was commissioned by the King Tiridates, the first of the Arshakuni dynasty of Armenia in the first century BC; after his return from a meeting with Nero in Rome. The construction date is estimated to be about 66 CE.

In the compound, the main point of interest is an inscribed stone called the Founding or Helios stone; on this stone Tiridates calls himself the Sun. Remnants of a palace he made for his sister, and third century remains of Roman baths are also present at the site.

The photos were taken on Sunday November 09, 2008. –Jalil Nozari.

The Helios Stone

Mithras artistic depiction by Robert Kavjian

Section 3: Religious Articles

MITHRAS SOL INVICTUS Invocation by M. Hajduk

(Reproduced Courtesy of Ancestral Folkways Magazine)

Unconquerable warrior

Face of the rising sun

Light eternal, immortal victory

Patron of the Legions

Lord of the divine hosts

Comrade, brother in arms

Guide us through the struggle

Initiator god, transcendent mystery

Son of the highest- Ahura Mazda

Bearing the radiance of the heavens

Enshrined in the stars of the firmament

Lord of the wide pastures

Light of the Aryans

We worship you with sacred fire

Atop highest plains

Ignite the divine spark within our souls

See us through all battles

Against the sons of decay

Lead us to a new dawn

Fill us with your Sun.

Ode to Aphrodite by Sappho, translated by Harita Meenee

Immortal Aphrodite in your flowered robe, crafty daughter of Zeus, I beg you,
Lady, don't torment my soul with distress and sorrow.

Come here as in past times, hearing from afar my cry,
you paid heed and left your father's palace, yoking your gold chariot

you arrived; lovely swift sparrows brought you on dark earth
flapping hard their wings from sky through ether.

Instantly they came; and you, a smile on your immortal face, oh blessed goddess,
you asked what I have suffered once more, why I called

you and what my frenzied heart most wants to happen. Who again do you long for?
Who should Persuasion bring to your love? Who wrongs you, Sappho?

Because if she avoids you, soon she'll pursue you, if she doesn't accept your gifts, she'll offer hers,
if she doesn't love you, soon she will though she may not want to.

Come to me once more and free me from painful thoughts,
what my soul desires, fulfill and become, yourself, my ally.

About the translator:

Harita Meenee is a Greek independent scholar of classical studies and women's history. She has presented cultural TV programs and has lectured at universities in Greece and the US. She is the author of four books, as well as of numerous articles published in Greek, British and American magazines and journals.

Website: www.hmeenee.com

Norooz Phiroze by Farida Bamji

Power of a Smile

Makes worries and woes

Like the snow melts away

Radiating happiness

The sadness, the tears

Instantly fade away

the Power of love is

A gigantic tsunami

Which engulfs all creations

Hidden in narrow crevices

or darkest of caves!

Zoroastrianism is like

Majestic Niagara Falls

Who's Pristine Teachings

Thunders as it gushes

Forth below into

The wide open sea

Creating a beautiful rippling effect

 As Crystal Clear Message

Gently meanders to

Distant shores "Equally"

Another new day

Another New Year

It's what lies ahead

We certainly do fear

If the Message

Were to be spread

Like the way it is

The fear of the

Unknown would disappear

But…till then

Let me wish you all

A Very Happy New Year!!!

More of Farida Bamji's work can be seen at:
1. http://groups.msn.com/ZoroastrianPoetryGroup
2. http://groups.msn.com/creatingawareness
3. http://groups.msn.com/ahunavargroup

Disappearing Shrines by S. David

Once upon a time,
No, not a fairy tale
Nor even a myth;
Once upon a time,
Across the high steppe,
The vast plateau,
Many fire shrines lit
The nights, burning too,
Through the days,
For the fires were to be
Eternal, as long as
The People rode.
And The People, the
Glorious People now gone
So long ago, carried
The God's symbols
On their migrations.
Traveling across and
Down from the heights
To green, wooded
Valleys below where
Their lives became
Ease and sloth and
They multiplied
And deserted
Or converted
Or perverted
Or forgot
And the God
Remembered and
Let them go.

Moving Shrines by S. David

Across the high plateau,
They rode so long ago;
Six, seven thousand years
Would pass and still the
Fire lasts,
Never to go out, handed
From elder to younger and
As each aged, still, again,
The flame would pass,
Sacred, unfailing until
The last was gone
Down to the lush valleys.
Still, they brought the
Flame and the God's Name.
Still, the God Is
And being the Light
And the Shadow,
Still, the God remains.
Ten thousand
Sobriquets,
Yet, the Same;
Flux, change,
Still, the Same.
History flees,

Still, He is Light,
Lord of Truth and
Goodly pastures.
Still, there are many
Knowing, remembering,
Calling His Name.

Brief Biography of S. David:

www.theskaldicsoul.com

I was born to a Canadian father and an American mother. I graduated Stuyvesant H.S. and attended a number of colleges, but graduated from Brooklyn College. Further graduate work completed at CUNY G.C. and a number of other places. While doing Graduate work, taught Sociology at various area colleges (12 years), drove a truck full time (8 years). I founded and was Executive Director of a Local Development Corporation and a local Historical society, also edited of several newsletters. Afterwards I taught JHS mathematics and social studies over the next 20 years. I hosted two Readings, Ozzie's (8 years) and The Tea Lounge (1+ years). I reside in Brooklyn with 3 dogs, too many books and Much music. Poetry Published in

Pivot	Medicinal Purposes
Rattapallax	N.Y. Nights
Bootface	The Green Gnome
Haiku Headlines	G
Nomad's Choir	The Browser

Video Reading: Sdavid.blip.tv   [at WAH Art Salon show of 2 24 08]

The Sleeping Lord by Katherine Sutherland

Hail to the sleeping Lord of the Land,
whose forehead is radiant with inner light,
who rests with morning in his right hand,
and calls to bring forth summer's might.

His body is strong and fortified,
in care of the living turning wheel,
and his rising cannot be denied,
as up through the earth the new seeds feel

their way through the slumbering form,
of the Lord recumbent in his dreams,
in the folded strata of rocks transformed
down ages through which wisdom streams.

And narrowed now, our eyes await him,
to help him to rise from a long wide bed,
where over the horizon he can brim
and ascend to the skies in a blaze of red.

Katherine Sutherland is a poet and author, her forthcoming collection *Underworld,* a reworking of the Persephone myth, will be published in 2009.

The right handed handshake of the Gods by Payam Nabarz

The debate about the origins of the Roman Mithras continues, and, while it is clear that the Roman Cult of Mithras was a syncretic religion using elements of Greek, Roman, and Persian cultures; it is less clear how influential different elements were in the production of the final Roman Cult. One aspect worth considering in the debate is the parallel between the act of the handshake, as seen in both the Persian Mithra and the Roman Mithras traditions. In modern times, shaking hands with the right hand is generally viewed as a sign of trust, as it shows no weapon is being held in the weapon bearing hand.

The oldest forms of handshakes were practiced by Babylonian Kings ca 1800 BCE, who had to 'take the hands of Marduk' before assuming the throne. According to Sir J. Frazer in The Golden Bough: 'At Babylon, within historical times, the tenure of the Kingly office was in practice lifelong, yet in theory it would seem to have been merely annual. For every year at the festival of Zagmuk the king had to renew his power by seizing the hands of the image of Marduk in his great temple of Esagil at Babylon. Even when Babylon passed under the power of Assyria, the monarchs of that country were expected to legalise their claim to the throne every year by coming to Babylon and performing the ancient ceremony at the New Year festival.'[1]

Another example Babylonian handshake is seen in the figure of Marduk-zakir-shumi of Babylon 703 BC (right) and Shalmaneser III (left) enacting a peace pact by shaking their right hands.[2]

The earliest mention of Mithra is on a 14th century BCE clay tablet, where he is the guarantor of an agreement between the Hittites and Mitanni. Mithra is the god of contracts and agreement, his name in Avestan means Treaty or Contract.

Antiochus I of Commagene, ca69 to ca31 BCE, on the Nemrud Dagh is shown **shaking his right hand with Mithra's right hand**. Mithra has his radiant crown and his Phrygian looking cap and cloak on his shoulders. Mithra in his left hand holds the *Barsom* the sacred twigs, as he is described as doing in the Zoroastrian Avesta. This right handed handshake between the King and Mithra back in ca50 BCE might seem trivial at first, after all Antiochus I also shakes hands with other deities at Nemrud Dagh including Ahura Mazda as well as Mithra. However, Mithra means 'contract'; he is the god of agreements and oaths, a point also mentioned by Professor Clauss: 'Mithra was god of the oath, protector of oaths. He was god of good faith, of agreements, of loyalty. Plutarch has an anecdote of how the Great King reminded one of his servants that he had bound himself to loyalty by **shaking hands** and by swearing by Mithra: Tell me (the truth), keeping faith with the light of Mithra and the King's **right hand**' (*Vit Alex 30.8*). -Manfred Clauss, *The Roman Cult of Mithras: The God and His Mysteries*.[3]

Figure: King Antiochus and Mithra.
Bas-relief of the colossal temple built by Antiochus I. of Commagene, 69-31 BCE, on the Nemrud Dagh, in the Taurus Mountains. (From *The Mysteries of Mithra*, by Franz Cumont. 1903. New York: Dover, 1956.) [4]

Figure: King Antiochus and Ahura-Mazda.
Bas-relief of the temple of Antiochus I. of Commagene, 69-34 BCE., on the Nemrud Dagh, in the Taurus Mountains. (From *The Mysteries of Mithra*, by Franz Cumont. 1903 .New York: Dover, 1956.[5]

Figure: Relief from Taq-e Bostan near Kermanshah, Iran. Photo by Philippe Chavin.⁶

Relief from Taq-e Bostan near Kermanshah, Iran, showing the investiture scene of Ardashir II (379–383 CE) of the Sasanian Empire. In middle the king is being given the right to rule, the divine kingship by Ahura Mazda, who hands the diadem with his right hand to the king's right hand. The two stand on a prostrate enemy. On the left is Mithra, wearing a crown of sun-rays, holding holy barsom twigs, and standing on a sacred lotus flower, he is also giving his blessings to his rule. One of duties of Mithra was to protect the Kingly Fortune or Divine Glory (*khvarnah* or *Farr*). The hymn to Mithra (Yasht 10) speaks of the divinity as the bestower of *khvarnah*.

The above examples show how in the ancient Middle Eastern Empires, the shaking of hands with the gods allowed the divine right of Kingship to be bestowed on the Kings by physical contact with a representation of the deity. This is a divine contract being formed when the handshake takes place, be it a peace treaty or the giving of the right to rule. The act transforms the person to stand in line with the Gods.

The divine handshake is taken from the Persian Mithra to the Roman Mithras; however, before examining this there are several other examples of right handed handshakes that need to be examined.

An example kindly provided by Dorjegiza is from the poem of Parmenides (5th century BCE), this is part of an initiate's journey from darkness to light, while in a chariot, in the company of the daughters of the Sun, he eventually reaches a temple of an unnamed goddess who enters into dialogue with him:
'(Line 20) sockets fastened with rivets and nails. Straight through them, on the broad way, did the maidens guide the horses and the car,
and the goddess greeted me kindly, and took **my right hand in hers,** and spake to me these words: -
Welcome, noble youth, that comest to my abode on the car
that bears thee tended by immortal charioteers!'
    -English translation by John Burnet (1892)[7]

Another example kindly provided Capanellius is a portrayal of Isis receiving Io with a right handed handshake (Temple of Isis, Pompeii)[8] 'Having thus settled in Egypt, Io made a statue of Demeter, and this goddess was then called Isis. And after that, the Egyptians also gave Io the name Isis, and Io-Isis, they say, was made a Goddess by Zeus.'[8] The handshake links the two Goddesses together, in a way a contract is formed, and they are now Io-Isis.

The paper *The Significance of the Handshake Motif in Classical Funerary Art* by Glenys Davies (American Journal of Archaeology, Vol. 89, No. 4. (Oct., 1985), pp. 627-640) provides further examples: 'The handshake appears in mythological scenes on a number of vases of the Archaic and Classical period. Many such scenes of the late archaic period involve Herakles: he is shown shaking hands with Athena on both black- and red-figure vases where the scene represents the acceptance of Herakles as an equal by the gods, and, in particular, his comradeship with Athena. Slightly later, as one might expect, the focus switches from Herakles to Theseus. On Early Classical red-figure vases Theseus is represented linking right hands with his father, Poseidon, again presumably to indicate Theseus' exalted status……The handshake also appears in the background of two paintings of the rescue of Andromeda, between Perseus and Andromeda's father Cepheu… and … There are also sporadic examples of the *dextrarum iunctio* used to link the deceased with his/her psychopompo as on a wall painting from Iserniag where the deceased is shown shaking hands with Mercury. The idea that the psychopompos leads the dead to a better life with the *dextrarum iunctio* is more explicitly stated in a painting in the tomb of Vibia on the Via Latinaos: there, a "good angel" leads Vibia by the right hand through an archway to the banquet of the blessed…..When used in a funerary context the handshake seems to have been associated especially with Hercules as a rescuing hero, and, to a lesser extent, with Mercury as psychopompos.'[9]

To come back to the divine handshake being taken from the Persian Mithra to the Roman Mithras, the Mithraic handshake was part of the initiatory rite, an act that connected the initiates to Mithras as well as fellow initiates.

Figure: Bas-relief fragment from Virunum in central Europe. (From *The Mysteries of Mithra*, by Franz Cumont. 1903. New York: Dover, 1956.) [10]

The Bas-relief fragment from Virunum in central Europe, shows scenes from Mithras' life, including (from bottom to top): smiting the rock from which the water flowed; holding the leg of the bull in his right hand and placing his left on Sun's head, the investiture of the Sun with his halo; Mithras and Sun **shaking right hands**; Mithras and the Sun in the chariot, showing their ascension to the sky.

Figure: Grand Mithraic bas-relief of Heddernheim, Germany. (From *The Mysteries of Mithra*, by Franz Cumont. 1903. New York: Dover, 1956.)[11]

The investiture scene towards the top right shows Mithras and the Sun **shaking right hands** while sun is kneeling.

Mithra is described as the Lord of wide pastures, the lord of truth and contracts. The custom of shaking hands when greeting a friend or after a business deal perhaps originated from the religious mysteries, as a sign of not carrying a weapon, and of trust. The depiction of Mithra shaking hands (right hands) with the Syrian King Antiochus in the first century BCE, is as a sign of the transfer of divine power from God to his earthly representative and sealing the divine 'contract'. In the Roman cult of Mithras a number of relief show Mithras and Sol shaking their right hands (dexiosis); and Mithraic initiates were termed *syndexioi*, 'those who have been united by a handshake' (with the Father). The handshake is also mentioned in Proficentius's poem from Rome, on the occasion of building his Mithraeum:

This spot is blessed, holy, observant and bounteous:
Mithras marked it, and made known to
Proficentius, Father of the mysteries,
That he should build and dedicate a Cave to him;
And he has accomplished swiftly, tirelessly, this dear task
That under such protection he began, desirous
That the **Hand-shaken** might make their vows joyfully forever.
These poor lines Proficentius composed,
Most worth Father of Mithras.
-Manfred Clauss, *The Roman Cult of Mithras: The God and His Mysteries* [12]

The Christian writer Firmicus Maternus (fourth century CE) referred to a Roman follower of Mithras as *mysta booklopies, syndexie patros agauou* (initiate of cattle-rustling, companion by **handclasp** of an illustrious father). -Marvin Meyer, *The Ancient Mysteries: A Sourcebook of Sacred Texts* [13]

In the Mithras Liturgy we read about Mithras as having 'a bright appearance, youthful, golden-haired, with a white tunic and a golden crown and trousers, and holding **in his right hand** a golden shoulder of a young bull: this is the Bear which moves and turns heaven around, moving upward and downward in accordance with the hour.' [14]

The right hand of Mithras moves the heavens, confers 'Divine Glory' to Kings and initiates of his mysteries, and binds them in a divine contract with the gods. The Mithraic handshake was a spiritual seal of agreement and the transfer of an initiatory line. The idea is seen in the Roman cult of Mithras with the same significance and connotations as the Persian Mithra.

We see this act of the divine right handed handshake down the ages, in Babylonian, Assyrian, Hittites, Mitanni, Commagene, Persian, Greek, Egyptian, and Roman religions.

It is worth noting that there are many initiatory systems still in practice today which use the right handed handshake as part of their mysteries. For example the Freemasons and some Sufis have their own special right-handed handshake as part of their initiation and becoming part of the initiatory line. This of course is the connection with the magical 'right-hand path' (the right hand pillar on the Kabbalistic Tree of Life and the RHP in Hinduism) and its deeper meaning of having shaken the right hand of the gods and becoming connected to the gods. The act of handshaking in business meetings is perhaps the most popular sign of a Mithraic act (lord of the contract) surviving to the modern day.

Author Biography:

Payam Nabarz is author of *The Mysteries of Mithras: The Pagan Belief That Shaped the Christian World* (Inner Traditions, 2005), *The Persian Mar Nameh: The Zoroastrian Book of the Snake Omens & Calendar* (Twin Serpents, 2006), and *Divine Comedy of Neophyte Corax and Goddess Morrigan* (Web of Wyrd, 2008). He is also editor of *Mithras Reader*. For further info visit: http://www.myspace.com/nabarz

References:

1. http://www.sacred-texts.com/pag/frazer/gb02403.htm
2. http://prophetess.lstc.edu/~rklein/images/shalthe3.jpg reproduced here with kind permission of Prof Ralph W.Klein.
3. Manfred Clauss, The Roman Cult of Mithras: The God and His Mysteries (Edinburgh, Scotland: Edinburgh University Press, 2000), p4.
4. The Mysteries of Mithra, by Franz Cumont. New York: Dover, 1956. [Originally published in 1903 by Open Court Publishing, London.] Also available online: http://www.sacred-texts.com/cla/mom/
5. *The Mysteries of Mithra*, by Franz Cumont. New York: Dover, 1956. [Originally published in 1903 by Open Court Publishing, London.]

6. http://commons.wikimedia.org/wiki/Image:Taq-e_Bostan_-_High-relief_of_Ardeshir_II_investiture.jpg Photo by 'Philippe Chavin' reproduced here with his kind permission.
7. English translation by John Burnet (1892) http://philoctetes.free.fr/parmenidesunicode.htm
8. http://www.maicar.com/GML/Io.html
9. *The Significance of the Handshake Motif in Classical Funerary Art* by Glenys Davies (American Journal of Archaeology, Vol. 89, No. 4. (Oct., 1985), pp. 627-640.
10. *The Mysteries of Mithra*, by Franz Cumont. New York: Dover, 1956. [Originally published in 1903 by Open Court Publishing, London.]
11. *The Mysteries of Mithra*, by Franz Cumont. New York: Dover, 1956. [Originally published in 1903 by Open Court Publishing, London.])
12. Manfred Clauss, *The Roman Cult of Mithras: The God and His Mysteries* (Edinburgh, Scotland: Edinburgh University Press, 2000), p42.
13. Marvin Meyer, *The Ancient Mysteries: A Sourcebook of Sacred Texts* (Philadelphia: University of Pennsylvania Press, 1987), p208.
14. Marvin Meyer, *The Ancient Mysteries: A Sourcebook of Sacred Texts* (Philadelphia: University of Pennsylvania Press, 1987), p218.

Book Reviews

Beck, R. The Religion of the Mithras Cult in the Roman Empire. Mysteries of the Unconquered Sun. *Review by: Dr. Israel Campos Méndez.*

New York: Oxford University Press, 2006. Pp. xiii+285. Hardcover. ISBN. 0198140894.

Dr. Israel Campos Méndez, is based at University of Las Palmas of Gran Canaria, Spain.

The professional career of R. Beck in the study of Mithraism is long and quite prolific. In fact, R. Beck along with the three other scholars to whom this book is dedicated (R. Gordon, J. Hinnells and L. Martin) are among the main contributors to the progress in the understanding of the cult of Mithra achieved in the second half of the twentieth century, after the seminal works of F. Cumont and M.J. Vermaseren. This book should be read in the context of R. Beck's maturity and his ability to perform an overall interpretation of Mithraism in order to offer several interesting developments on some of the most obscure points of the Mithraic Cult.

R. Beck's objective is to redirect the investigation that has been done on the Mithraic Mysteries until now. To do so, the book focuses on two main controversial issues already introduced in previous studies: a) the excessive prominence given to the interpretation of the topic of iconography as a vehicle for the reconstruction of the Mithraic doctrine, and, by contrasts, b) the secondary place given to the mithraeum as compared to the other elements of the cult. R. Beck provides an interesting novelty: he tries to re-evaluate the Mithraic temple as one of the protagonists in Mithraism, and hence the importance that must be accorded to the elements that are present in it, as a means of rebuilding the Mithraic doctrine.

The point that makes this reconsideration possible is R. Beck's interest to increase the value of Porphyry's De Antro. This classical text is to be considered from a new perspective in order to value the information about the symbolic significance of the mithraeum. According to the author, each of the elements which have been arranged in the mithraea respond to a defined purpose, as they are part of an 'own language' whose interpretation keys were transmitted to the Mithraic initiated in the process of joining the community. Within this 'own language' Beck aligns with the branch of modern research, which tends to give a higher profile to the astrological subject within the theological and doctrinal Mithraic corpus. In the middle of this discourse, other aspects seem to be abandoned, for example, the question of the origin of the Mithraic iconography presented inside the Mithraea, and the possible connections with Persia or other religious traditions.

In general, the plan of the work appears very clear, but its conclusions do not necessarily help to systematize the author's main contributions. The arrangement of chapters and distribution of their contents are somewhat confusing. Sometimes, the book offers the information in a schematic way, however an excessive subdivision in the chapters that make it hard to follow the main points. As a result, instead of providing plain explanations, these subdivisions tend to dilute the argumentative discourse. The language is occasionally obscure and rambling, which makes some chapters difficult to read and forcing more than one reading to fully understand the ideas transmitted.

R. Beck's new book is a worthwhile read; the author has managed to communicate several original and new intuitions on some dark points of this Ancient Religion, but we are also convinced that R. Beck could have opted for a simpler and more direct way to present these points. This book is not written with an ordinary group of readers interested in ancient mystery religions in mind; it is a deep academic essay. Even those scholars with a level of knowledge in this subject will need some serenity and patience in order to gain a complete understanding of the arguments proposed in this book.

Adverts

ANCESTRAL FOLKWAYS
A Journal of Indo-European Myth, Culture, and Religion
VOLUME I, ISSUE 2

Featured Articles of Interest Include:

* Tyr: Primordial Indo-Germanic Chieftain and Sky Father, by Matt Hajduk
* The Allegorical Hero and the Initiatory Quest for Virtue, by Lesley Madytinou
* Of Wolves and Men: The Berserker and the Vratya, by Gwendolyn Toynton
* Slavic Family Rituals, by Zerca Rafal Merski
* Teufelskraut-- Devil's Herb, by Amy Ahlberg-Venezia
* Music Reviews

Published Biannually
$15.00 per Individual Issue/ $28.00 Year Subscription within United States (shipping included)
PLEASE NOTE SPECIAL RATE FOR INCARCERATED READERS (USA): $10.00 issue/ $18.00 year
International Rates are $21.00 per Individual Issue/ $40.00 Year Subscription (shipping included)
Discounted pdf digital version $3.00 per Issue/ $5.00 Subscription

Payment is accepted via cash, check or money order payable to:
"Ancestral Folkways LLC", PO Box 1221, Boston, MA 02134, USA
(For online PayPal payments, please direct them to: ancestral_folkways@hotmail.com)

Past Preservers is in search of Experts, Presenters, Researchers and your Projects and Ideas.

Past Preservers is happy to announce that we are now seeking experts and advanced students to help in the production of major documentary projects to be filmed in Egypt and elsewhere.

We are looking for rising specialists in all areas of Egyptology, archaeology, and related areas of historical study who will readily and energetically share their knowledge and enthusiasm for their subject, both on camera and off it, as either "talking heads" in television documentaries or as researchers behind the scenes.

This exciting work will afford the opportunity to learn in a hands-on way how the sciences of archaeology and historical analysis are conveyed through the various media of documentary television and film, and promises to be an interesting way to gain exposure in the field and see how documentaries are actually made.

Additionally, we welcome fresh ideas for media projects and are eager to help our talent pursue new avenues of research and presentation; a major part of Past Preservers job is to provide the best possible representation and support for a new concept or project as it makes its way from mere suggestion to fully fleshed-out production, and we hope you will feel welcome in bringing forward your best and brightest.

If interested, please send a current CV, including date of birth, nationality, and mention of any previous experience working in the media, along with a photograph of you, to: sam@pastpreservers.com

Sol Invictus: The God Tarot

By Kim Huggens and Nic Phillips

www.godtarot.com

GOD. Many faces, many forms, many mysteries...

At last the traditional Tarot archetypes are expressed and explored through the esoteric myths, fantastical tales, true stories, and age old legends of the Divine Masculine.

Sol Invictus: The God Tarot provides priceless information and original artwork to guide you into the tapestry of universal mythical motifs as expressed in the tales of Gods, heroes, saints, and figures from history, legends, and folklore. Here, the *Sol Invictus Tarot* introduces all-male deities to the archetypal world of Tarot for the first time, mingling the timeless wisdom of mythical themes with the practicality and beauty of the Tarot. Includes:

- 78 original and fully illustrated, colourful Tarot cards
- An in-depth 264-page companion guide that includes interpretations, academic research, and myths;
- And 10 revealing layouts for successful Tarot spreads

Ancient Iran by Massoume Price

Book: Hardcover | 8.77 x 11.18in | 72 pages | ISBN 978-0-9809714-0-8 | July 2008 | 8 + years

Winner of the Moonbeam Children's Book Awards bronze medal for one of the best multicultural non-fiction books in 2008.

Description

Discover the great civilizations of the Iranian plateau - from the Burnt City in Sistan & Baluchistan in eastern Iran to the splendor of the Sasanian court in the legendary city of Cteisphon in modern Iraq. Spanning a 5,500-year period, this is the first book to document the ancient civilizations of the Iranian plateau in a pictorial format for children ages eight and up. The book provides a comprehensive and easy to read look at life in ancient Iran. It features unique items such as a 5000-year old textile fragment and an artificial eyeball from the Burnt City and stunning objects from the ancient ruins of Susa in southern Iran. Follow life at the magnificent palaces of the Persian nobles at Persepolis, labeled by the Greek historians as the wealthiest city under the sun.

Find out how the ancient Iranians lived, what they ate, how they were entertained and what they believed in. Trace the origin of Iranian languages and the development of Iranian scripts over the centuries. Discover the life of women and children and view fantastic jewelry the wealthy nobles, both male and female, wore for adornment. Follow the path of Alexander and the defeat of his heirs, the Seleucids, by the master archers the Parthians who ruled Iran for almost 500 years and stopped Roman advances into the Near East. Learn about the splendor of the Sasanian court and its contribution to the arts, textiles and music of the Near East for centuries, even after its demise in the 7th century.

Mithras Reader Vol 1

This edition includes: Continuity and Change in the Cult of Mithra, by Dr. Israel Campos Mendez. Mithra and the warrior group Mithra and the Iranian words and images Introduction to Classes of Manichean, Mithraism and Sufiyeh, by Dr. Saloome Rostampoor. Entheos ho syros, polymathes ho phoinix: Neoplatonist approaches to religious practice in Iamblichus and Porphyry, by Sergio Knipe. Mithraism and Alchemy, by David Livingstone. Meeting Mithra, by Guya Vichi. Ode To Mithra, by Guya Vichi. Hymn to the Sun, by Katherine Sutherland. Mithras Liturgy with the Orphic Hymns, by Payam Nabarz.
ISBN-13: 978-1905524099.

www.ingramcontent.com/pod-product-compliance
Lightning Source LLC
Chambersburg PA
CBHW071626170426
43195CB00038B/2147